"Ike has given us a gift in *Good B*  the pain of childhood trauma t Ike shows us that healing and tr As someone who has spent decades working through my own childhood trauma and its impact on my relationships, I wish I had read this book earlier. Ike not only inspires us to believe that change is possible, but he also offers actual practices and exercises that lead to healthy relationships."

Christine Caine, founder of A21 and Propel Women

" 'The heart of this book is the desire to see the pain of your difficult childhood redeemed.' This excerpt captures not only the essence of this book but also the deep longing so many have. As a pastor, I'm routinely in conversation with adults who have spent so much time trying to make sense of their childhoods. This is why Ike Miller's work is a great gift. He offers powerful storytelling, poignant insights, and a hope-filled vision of healing that often feels elusive. I'm grateful for this book!"

Rich Villodas, lead pastor of New Life Fellowship and author of *Good and Beautiful and Kind*

"No one outmaneuvers the complexities of their childhood, but *Good Baggage* provides clarity and hope in its aftermath. Ike Miller has masterfully addressed our real questions, offered powerful perspectives, and given us tools to move forward. This book is so critical for pastors and leaders, it should be their next read and on their recommended resource list—it's on mine."

Lisa Whittle, author of *God Knows*, Bible teacher, podcast host

"Ike has written an important book. It's important because he is going to help you unpack the baggage of your past. Surprisingly, by loving transformationally, you will see that what you thought was going to break you, Jesus will use to remake you."

Dr. Derwin L. Gray, cofounder and lead pastor of Transformation Church and author of the bestselling *The Good Life*

"One of the most important things we can do for our friends and our families, for the churches we lead, and for the people we work with and for is to unpack the bags we carry. A healthier you is good for you and good for the world. The most significant gift in these pages is a guide who has done the work and is taking the risk of vulnerability to help us do the same. With pastoral tenderness, Ike helps us unpack each learned behavior or reflex or tendency from our childhood and families of origin. He gives us the tools and the vocabulary to name and sort them. But best of all, he shows us how Jesus can reclaim and redeem them, bringing beauty from ashes."

Glenn Packiam, lead pastor of Rockharbor Church and author of *The Resilient Pastor* and *The Intentional Year*

"In a well-researched journey, Ike Miller takes the concept of 'when life gives you lemons' and applies it to what no one has control over—childhood family distress and trauma. Using sound psychology and personal experiences, Ike shows how growing up with family dysfunction can both hinder and encourage relationships in adulthood. From instability in identity to a fierce loyalty for others, Ike looks at both sides of the situation—what needs to be helped and what has been gained from being part of a family that struggled. No family is perfect. Understanding how our family dynamic has affected us can point us in the direction of fixing what is broken and accessing tools we may not have known we had."

Shannon Plate, Licensed Clinical Professional Counselor, author of *Care Talk*

GOOD
BAGGAGE

GOOD BAGGAGE

HOW YOUR DIFFICULT CHILDHOOD PREPARED YOU FOR HEALTHY RELATIONSHIPS

IKE MILLER

BakerBooks
a division of Baker Publishing Group
Grand Rapids, Michigan

Published by Baker Books
a division of Baker Publishing Group
Grand Rapids, Michigan
www.bakerbooks.com

Printed in the United States of America

Library of Congress Cataloging-in-Publication Data
Names: Miller, Ike, 1985– author.
Title: Good baggage : how your difficult childhood prepared you for healthy relationships / Ike Miller.
Description: Grand Rapids, Michigan : Baker Books, a division of Baker Publishing Group, [2023]
Identifiers: LCCN 2022051405 | ISBN 9781540902863 (paperback) | ISBN 9781540903624 (casebound) | ISBN 9781493443307 (ebook)
Subjects: LCSH: Interpersonal relations.
Classification: LCC HM1106 .M53 2023 | DDC 302—dc23/eng/20221222
LC record available at https://lccn.loc.gov/2022051405

Unless otherwise indicated, Scripture quotations have been taken from the Christian Standard Bible®, copyright © 2017 by Holman Bible Publishers. Used by permission. Christian Standard Bible® and CSB® are federally registered trademarks of Holman Bible Publishers.

Scripture quotations labeled ESV are from The Holy Bible, English Standard Version® (ESV®), copyright © 2001 by Crossway, a publishing ministry of Good News Publishers. Used by permission. All rights reserved. ESV Text Edition: 2016

Scripture quotations labeled NIV are from THE HOLY BIBLE, NEW INTERNATIONAL VERSION®, NIV® Copyright © 1973, 1978, 1984, 2011 by Biblica, Inc.® Used by permission. All rights reserved worldwide.

Some names and identifying details have been changed to protect the privacy of individuals.

This publication is intended to provide helpful and informative material on the subjects addressed. Readers should consult their personal health professionals before adopting any of the suggestions in this book or drawing inferences from it. The author and publisher expressly disclaim responsibility for any adverse effects arising from the use or application of the information contained in this book.

Published in association with the Bindery Agency, www.TheBinderyAgency.com.

Baker Publishing Group publications use paper produced from sustainable forestry practices and post-consumer waste whenever possible.

23 24 25 26 27 28 29   7 6 5 4 3 2 1

TO ISAAC, COEN, AND SADIE.
THIS WORK, I DO FOR YOU.

CONTENTS

FOREWORD

When I was seventeen years old, I played on my high school's baseball team. We were ranked nationally and had a chance to win the state championship (spoiler alert: we lost in the championship).

But during a routine scrimmage practice that year, when I was playing center field, my buddy hit a deep fly ball in the gap. I began running as fast as I could, tracking it down. I remember it looking like it was going to be just out of reach, and I might need to dive.

And so I did.

For about three seconds I felt like superman as I leapt through the sky—and caught the ball! It was incredible. Then I crash-landed on the grass.

And I heard one of the loudest cracks I've ever heard.

I didn't feel pain right away, but when I stood up and tried to lift my right arm, I physically wasn't able to. Long story short, I completely shattered my collarbone and dislocated my shoulder—and worst of all, my bone was sticking out of my right shoulder.

Then the pain came. Searing and sharp. I remember almost passing out from how painful it was. And for weeks it was like that. So tender, sensitive, and sharp.

Because that's what a wound is. A present injury that hasn't healed yet. And a *present wound* has very specific characteristics.

1. It can become infected and continue to get worse.
2. It is usually covered or hidden by a bandage or clothing.
3. It is highly sensitive to pain, and we usually cringe or retract if someone gets close to it.

Now, think about how fundamentally different a scar is from a wound. If a wound is *properly* healed, it becomes a scar. And scars are very, very different.

Scars have their own specific characteristics too.

1. They are no longer vulnerable to further festering or infection.
2. We don't cover the scar under a bandage (in fact, we usually "show" people!).
3. It is no longer painful and tells a specific story.

When I hurt my collarbone and shoulder, after a few months and two metal plates and eleven screws, it became a scar. And instead of hiding the wound, I went around in a classic high school bro way saying, "Dude, look what happened!"

The scar/wound metaphor is one I couldn't stop thinking about when I was reading Ike's words in this book. He so brilliantly and thoughtfully lays out a road map to show

how a difficult circumstance can, if healed properly, actually become a superpower.

Think about Jesus. What did he still show in his resurrected body? His perfect body? He showed scars. Meaning Jesus forever will have those scars when he easily could've had them removed in the resurrection as signs of "blemish." But I think they are there forever in Jesus's body because that's who he is. A God who is in the business of making wounds scars, and one who wants to get glory from our stories forever.

Be the one who wants to get glory from our stories forever.

—Jefferson Bethke

INTRODUCTION

GOOD BAGGAGE?

As a single guy in my early twenties, I had a thought many of us share: "I hope the person I marry doesn't have a ton of baggage."

Just a couple of years later, I'd eat my words. I wasn't married long before discovering I had plenty of baggage for the both of us. But in working through my baggage, I learned a crucial truth—the truth at the heart of this book.

My own story involves a family whose dysfunction centered around my father's disease. In his case, the condition was alcoholism. It drove brokenness in every relationship in our family and ultimately ended my parents' marriage. It would take my becoming a husband, having children, and years of processing to fully grasp the dysfunction's repercussions.

Maybe like me, you grew up amid a painful reality that entailed traumatic experiences. This book is for all of us who experienced dysfunction in our family of origin or difficulty in our childhood.

Dysfunctional families and difficult childhoods come in many forms. Dysfunctional families are marked by the pervasive presence of conflict and instability. Some form of abuse or neglect is often present, and the dysfunction can be due to addiction, codependency, or untreated mental illness. The defining traits of dysfunctional families are poor communication, perfectionism, absence of empathy, controlling tendencies, and excessive criticism.[1]

A difficult childhood may not be due to conflict or substance use. It could be due to an emotionally immature, distant, or physically ill parent. Maybe the illness of a family member consumed the family and shaped how you saw yourself and the world. Difficult childhoods can also be the result of "secondhand" dysfunction. Maybe one or both of your parents grew up in a dysfunctional context, and though they were not abusive, controlling, or caught in addiction themselves, the impact of growing up in that context affected how they related to you, your siblings, and your other parent.

Although our difficult childhoods share much in common, each of our stories is deeply personal and unique to us. To honor this diversity in our stories, I'll use various terms to speak to our shared experience: childhoods in which things were not as they should be.

Whether we call it a dysfunctional family or a difficult childhood, it was an environment that would be toxic for anyone, much less a child moving through the critical stages of development. So it's important to acknowledge up front that the baggage we carry served a crucial purpose in our early lives—it helped us survive. We need to honor the work that our younger selves did. We must acknowledge that even if these coping mechanisms were unhealthy, they served a purpose—they kept us alive.

So instead, don't shame yourself or others for having created critical techniques to survive. Our work now is to understand why these skills no longer serve us as adults and what we need to do about them.

The Good News

In my experience, all we hear about are the ways our difficult childhood makes us bad at relationships. But the truth is, bad relationships in childhood do not predestine us to be bad at relationships ourselves. In fact, we came out of our difficult childhood with relational wisdom, emotional intelligence, and a hard-won level of awareness that comes only from having seen some things. Your difficult childhood prepared you for healthy relationships.

This may sound counterintuitive, illogical, or even absurd. But it's true. You may not have seen or experienced it yet, but it's in you, and that's what this book is about. There's a difference between *preparation* and *realization*. This book is about the process we must undergo to move from preparing for healthy relationships to realizing those relationships.

What matters most, however, isn't that we achieve complete healing—as if that were possible—but that we begin the process right now. Our relationships depend on it. Our difficult childhood has given us tools and raw materials. But now we need to learn how to leverage them.

Until we do that, we can perpetuate the harm we experienced in childhood. We will use the tools and materials we were given in all the wrong ways and with all the wrong people. We will hurt ourselves rather than heal. We will inflict greater wounds and cast blame where we ought to take responsibility.

The good news about baggage, the truth at the center of this book, is this: *it's not all bad.*

Baggage isn't just what makes us bad at relationships. Baggage is the pain we carry along with the lessons it's taught us. Nobody wants it, but the truth is, we've all got it. We've all experienced the pain of betrayal, dishonesty, rejection, and shame from relationships. But the pain we carry carries its own promises.

Our difficult childhood helped us pack some really good stuff into those bags. This book is about finding those good things and leveraging them to help our relationships flourish now.

How I Began to Discover the *Good* Baggage

About three months into married life, Sharon and I took a trip to Disney World. For context, Sharon grew up celebrating birthdays and significant milestones throughout her life there. She lives as though Disney is her birthright. I, however, had never been. Sharon put it to me this way: "If you're going to be married to me, you need to understand my love for Disney."

As we boarded the plane for Orlando, she was grinning from ear to ear. I said, "You're more excited about this than you were for our honeymoon!"

I expected her to at least feign denial. Instead, she simply replied, "It's a different kind of excited."

This told me everything I needed to know about her love for Disney.

We were a few days into our trip when I realized that in "the happiest place on earth," I wasn't very happy. I was miserable. I was putting on a show for Sharon, but I was lifeless on the inside. When we returned home from the trip, I shared with her what I'd experienced and wondered if I was dealing with some depression.

After my official diagnosis of depression, my "baggage-free" image began to crumble. I discovered I was bringing a lot to the relationship that hadn't been addressed.

I threw myself into books on adult children of dysfunctional families and how that had shaped me. I sought counseling and inner-healing prayer experiences, and I read extensively about spiritual, mental, and emotional health. I pursued graduate-level counseling studies and regularly participated in a twelve-step program for adult children of alcoholic/dysfunctional families.

I also studied ancient Christian practices in spirituality and their intersection with theology. In this process, I developed tools for investigating my inner world with the guidance of God's Spirit—tools I'm excited to share with you.

Out of this passion for pursuing a healthy relationship, my instinct was to address my depressive disorder head-on. I'd seen where things go when mental health struggles go unaddressed. I knew firsthand such things don't go away; they only grow. Pain doesn't die just because we bury it.

At that point, Sharon and I began meeting with a counselor regularly. It's one of the best decisions we've ever made for our relationship, and we've continued this discipline throughout our marriage. We kept going not because we had big problems, but because we didn't *want* big problems.

I often wonder if I would be as motivated to pursue healthy relationships if I hadn't experienced the pain of unhealthy ones in my childhood.

Redeeming Childhood

The heart of this book is the desire to see the pain of your difficult childhood redeemed. The things you went through, yes, they harmed you. But that doesn't have to be the end of your story. I want to identify the gifts those hard things gave you and help you learn to leverage them for the kind of relationships you've always wanted.

We'll begin by looking at some big questions you may never have asked out loud but that have been an ache in your soul all your life: Why does it feel like nothing is ever *really* okay? What's a normal relationship anyway? And most importantly, can anything good come of this baggage I'm carrying?

Once you've discovered there is good news, we'll begin by addressing the bad news, meaning the ruthless cycle sabotaging our relationships: codependency, approval seeking, deception, and boundary issues. In codependency, we lose our sense of self, so approval-seeking becomes a means of creating an identity we believe others will love. When we burn out on seeking approval, we resort to deception to keep up appearances and protect ourselves from rejection. Boundaries are the proper form of relational protection, but our codependency won't allow us to enforce them. And so the cycle starts over again. We must break this ruthless cycle if we're going to realize the exceptional relationships we've been prepared for.

Then we get to the good news: six aspects of the good baggage our childhood put in us and how they can work together for the good of our relationships now.

Finally, we'll end with a couple of chapters that put this all together. One's on overcoming our obstacles to healthy relationships and the other's on how to start embracing our good baggage now.

I'm excited for the journey you're about to begin. There's some good stuff in your baggage, and I'm going to help you find it. Your difficult childhood prepared you for healthy relationships.

PT1 | THE UNSPOKEN QUESTIONS WE KEEP ASKING

Three common questions stir below the surface of our emotional worlds. Only when we name these questions can we begin to address the unrest they constantly cause in us.

The first two questions underlay many of the relational obstacles we face. Once we understand our subconscious struggle with these questions, we can begin to tackle these obstacles and achieve the objective of this book: learning to leverage our baggage for the good of our relationships.

We'll end the section with a question some of us still ask and others of us gave up hope on long ago: Can anything good come from what I've been through?

The answer we'll discover is the secret to maximizing everything this book has to offer: You and I live with an unrelenting passion to see our relationships go differently than the ones we experienced in our childhood.

1

IS ANYTHING EVER REALLY OKAY?

In July 2014, Sharon and I moved back to North Carolina after four years in Chicago. Sharon was a couple of months pregnant with our second child, and we were both finishing our dissertations. We moved back because North Carolina was where we wanted to be long-term. There was just one hiccup—we relocated before we got the final word on the job I was hoping to land. It was a stressful time for both of us.

We moved into our little, second-floor, two-bedroom apartment in Holly Springs and waited for our shipping pod with all our treasured possessions to arrive. We waited. And waited. On the day it finally came, it was your typical ninety-five-degree, 100-percent-humidity July day in North Carolina. I went to open the rolling door of our pod, only to find it was jammed. I got it open far enough to sneak my head in and awkwardly twist my neck to discover that one of our dining room chairs had shifted during transit and its foot was now firmly lodged in the rung of the rolling door.

You've got to be kidding me, I thought. *Not today . . .*

I wiped the sweat from my brow and went to work dislodging the chair. I fought the door for what felt like hours, making trip after trip into the apartment for yet another tool. Just as I was reaching my wit's end, it started to rain. That was the moment I broke. The sweat, the rain, and the tears all began to run down my face like tributaries rushing into a river.

I lost it. *Why does it always have to be hard? Why can't anything be easy? Why can't things ever be okay?*

This moment by the pod in the rain was a lot, to be sure. But honestly, it felt on par for life.

It's something that's real to many of us from dysfunctional families: the struggle to feel like things are ever *really* okay. This feeling is tough to bear when coupled with the sense that we're also the ones who should make it okay. Somehow, it's our responsibility to fix everything.

Sometimes things are okay, but that's only because we've constantly worked to keep them that way, and everything will fall apart if we stop. This isn't simply a lack of faith. It comes from us having played a stabilizing role in our dysfunctional family of origin. Now the part of stabilizer is ingrained into our beings. Unfortunately, as children, we couldn't keep things "okay" in our homes for long because they weren't really in our control anyway.

As adults, okay is never enough because we don't know what it feels like. Everyone tells us things are good, and we can see that, but we also believe things are more fragile than everyone thinks.

As it did for so many of us, the pandemic lockdown meant my whole family was at home all the time with nowhere to go and nothing to do. Sharon and I split our days between working and watching the kids. This meant long periods when I had all three kids to myself. As the days and weeks went by and the pressures and tensions of life mounted, I struggled to be present with them. I was irritable and lost my temper too quickly. I was watching them, but my mind was working on problems at work.

Things weren't okay at home. Things weren't okay at work. And things weren't okay within me.

My depression was resurfacing, and I was beginning to struggle with anxiety. The fact that things weren't okay was intensified by the guilt I felt for not being able to make things okay. The plan of care my psychiatrist prescribed included an as-needed antianxiety medication.

As the pandemic dragged on and the tensions in our world heightened, I took increasing amounts of my antianxiety medication to numb the pain I couldn't fix and silence the shame I felt for not being able to fix it. Eventually I developed an unhealthy relationship with my medication.

Sharon discovered my medication misuse in what I've come to call a moment of God's severe mercy. This forced the most difficult confession of all: *I was not okay.*

The Source of This False Belief

As I dug deeper to understand the source of this pressure to fix everything, I found that at the base of it was the false belief that everything depended on me. The truth is, this was a weight I wasn't made to carry. (This pressure is exacerbated if we come from a family system in which we couldn't trust a caregiver to nurture, protect, and meet our needs.)

I was suffering under the weight of an overinflated sense of how much things depended on me. In theological terms,

I was dealing with a less commonly discussed form of pride. It's not that I was boastful or thought too highly of myself. Instead, it was the kind of pride that says, "Only I can carry this. Otherwise, it will fall apart."

Now, pride often gets labeled as a deeply sinful problem, and for those of us who grew up in religious contexts, we equate sin with something that needs to be punished. This is an incomplete definition of sin.

This kind of pride doesn't arise from foolish arrogance. It comes from the extreme sense of responsibility we carry into everything we do—a sense of responsibility for more than we were meant to carry by ourselves.

In the original Greek, "sin" was an archery term. It meant to miss the mark. The "sin" of an arrow was the distance between where the arrow landed on a target and the bull's-eye of the target.

Theologically, this is used metaphorically to name the reality that creation has "missed the mark" of what it was created to be—things aren't as they should be. In this light, some sin is willful disobedience and rebellion against God. But a lot of our "missing the mark" is the outworking of our brokenness. Things aren't as they should be because broken people hurt us, and we're living out of the brokenness inflicted on us.

This isn't an excuse to say we aren't responsible for our actions and decisions. But a more robust view of salvation is that Christ didn't come only to take away punishment for our sins. He also came as the great physician to *heal us* of sin and its effects. This is an especially powerful correction to our theology for those of us who grew up under harsh and abusive punishment.

Not everything in us needs punishing. Some of what's broken in us needs healing.

In this framework, pride isn't exalting ourselves above others. Pride is the overinflated sense that *everything* depends on us. Granted, this isn't a feeling we chose. It's something that formed in us because of the dysfunction of our childhood. Nevertheless, it needs to be healed because it produces overwhelming pressure that leads to exhaustion and burnout. It needs healing not just for God's sake but also for ours.

The antidote to pride is still humility, but a kind of humility that's different from what we're used to. Humility is often defined as thinking lowly of ourselves. Coming from dysfunctional families, that "humility" seems to come naturally for many of us. Instead, Andrew Murray gives one of the most beautiful definitions of humility: humility is living from a place of complete dependence on God.[1]

On this reading, the sin of pride in the garden of Eden wasn't that Adam and Eve wanted to be equal with God. The sin of pride was believing they could make their lives better by adding to what God had already given them. They moved from complete dependence on God to relying on themselves. Along with that came fear, shame, and doubt about God's goodness. Murray writes that at this moment, "They fell from their high position."[2] At the moment they attempted to exalt themselves to the side of God, they fell from the lightness and freedom that came from dependence on him.

In our own lives, we may feel a need to "help God" a little. We might not put it that way, but the sense that nothing is ever okay unless we constantly work to make it okay betrays this deep-seated belief. To this mentality, Murray says that in false humility, we say, "I'm only a little bit." But to say we are a little bit is to say that God is not all. God is only "most." True humility is "the place of entire dependence on God," the simple sense of entire nothingness that leaves God free to be all.[3]

In humility, we remember that it all depends on God, and we live from a place of utter dependence on him.

Complicated by Stages of Intoxication

For those of us who grew up with a parent with alcoholism or substance abuse, this feeling that nothing was ever okay was exacerbated by the fact that we didn't yet understand the stages of intoxication.[4] This misunderstanding alone was a major contributing factor to our trauma as children.

Because of their limited awareness, children live with a sense of "omnipotence"—everything that happens around them is interpreted as a direct result of their actions. As children, this led us to believe that our parents' responses to us were about our actions rather than their level of inebriation.

A parent with an awful hangover might've responded to our request for a snack with great anger and disgust: "Why do you always need something from me?"[5]

However, within an hour or two, when they had resumed drinking, our parent might have replied, "Sure, buddy. What can I make for my favorite child?"

Without awareness of our parent's stage of intoxication, we assumed the change in response was due to *how* we asked the question. *From now on, I just need to ask the right way,* we concluded.

A while later, when they were in the happy drunk stage, our parent might've doted on us with hugs and high fives.

"You're so smart. I'm so proud of you! You know what? Tonight let's go celebrate YOU!" As a child, we were in heaven, unaware that this plan would change momentarily.

Finally, dinnertime came, and we said, "Let's go celebrate like you said, remember?" The parent, on the backside of the intoxication, replied, "Who would ever celebrate you?"

Without any awareness of the journey the parent had just gone on, we assumed we were the cause of both the positive and negative responses, and we internalized the guilt for causing the negative ones.

This led us, as children of such dysfunction, to be hyper-vigilant, overly conscientious, and self-critical, and to judge ourselves without mercy. We also concluded that we could control people with our actions if we figured out what they wanted from us.

Now, we experience great anxiety in our relationships because we fear that every occurrence of rejection, disapproval, disappointment, anger, or other adverse reaction is a direct reflection on us.

Although we now have an intellectual awareness that we aren't in control of everything, subconsciously we expect to be able to control everything. Or at least to fix it. When we learn that we have this subconscious belief that we can control others, we appreciate even more how our difficult childhood continues to affect us now.

Building a Cognitive Life Raft

In their book *After the Tears: Helping Adult Children of Alcoholics Heal Their Childhood Trauma*, Jane Middelton-Moz and Lorie Dwinell explain that an essential part of dealing with our trauma is building a "cognitive life raft."[6] The challenges of adult life in the aftermath of our childhoods can be every bit as overwhelming as floating in the open sea. Building a cognitive life raft means developing a clear understanding of what happened to us in our childhood and then using that understanding to better cope with the ongoing impact of our childhood. This includes understanding the characteristics we developed to survive and how they may now work against us. Most importantly, we must understand that we're not "crazy." Instead, we "are having a normal reaction to what was an abnormal and painful life."[7]

This cognitive life raft allows us to unload many of the messages, responsibilities, and beliefs about ourselves that we've been carrying for so long. These thoughts have been like weights upon our backs threatening to force us under. As we name these messages, responsibilities, and beliefs, we can take them off and throw them into the raft. This allows us to discover what's essential to our identity versus what was necessary for our survival as children.

Many of these beliefs about ourselves came from the roles we played in our dysfunctional family. If we played the caretaker role, for example, we might carry the belief that we're responsible for ensuring everything is okay. We may feel anxious and out of place when we don't have anyone to take care of. Once we can name that this was a role and not essential to our identity, we can take that weight from around our neck and throw it into the raft. Picture yourself doing this; you may feel lighter already!

This isn't to say we shouldn't ever take care of people. It just means we don't bear the weight of ensuring everyone is okay. We may enjoy taking care of others and find it to be meaningful work. But sometimes we take on this role for unhealthy, manipulative, or codependent reasons. The cognitive life raft allows us space to acknowledge this intellectually and then gradually come to accept it emotionally.

Using the Cognitive Life Raft

Here are a few ways to use the cognitive life raft that I've found most helpful. Try them out and adapt them for yourself. If one isn't helpful, that's okay. The important thing is to find what's most effective for unearthing what's operating below the surface in your own life.

Name the Messages, Responsibilities, and False Beliefs You Carry

A list of all the messages, responsibilities, and false beliefs you carry might include the following:

» If I'm not perfect, I'm worthless.
» "Fun and carefree" is not an option for me.
» I should be able to control the uncontrollable.
» Loyalty is always the best policy.
» I have to be superman/superwoman.
» If people really knew who I was, they would
  _____.
» I don't deserve their time, attention, or approval.
» I'm different from everyone else / no one understands me.
» All I know how to do is be impulsive.
» I'm just a screwup.

» No one will ever take me seriously.

» Why can't I do anything right?

» I'll never have a long-term relationship.

Think of Specific Moments When These Messages, Responsibilities, or False Beliefs Were Enacted

Can you think of a particular moment when you felt like you needed to step up? Why did you feel that way? Can you think of a moment you felt things would fall apart if you didn't perform perfectly? What consequences of failure did you fear? What would be the fallout of failing? Why did you feel so much pressure in that moment?

Utilize the "Five Whys" Tool

Our actions, reactions, and emotions are often just symptoms of what's going on deeper down within us. The "five whys" help us get at what that is.[8]

As the story goes, the five whys originated in Toyota automobile factories. Whenever there was a problem on the assembly-line floor, the manager would utilize the five whys to understand the root cause. For example, if windshield installation was consistently delayed, they wouldn't just go to that team member and tell them to work faster. They would ask the first why. It might go something like this:

First why: *Why are you having trouble installing windshields?*
Answer: The person in charge of prepping the windshields for me is delayed.
They would go and ask the second why: *Why are you late in prepping the windshields?*

Answer: The truck delivering windshields is consistently late.

They would then ask the third why: *Why are the windshield shipments late?*

Answer: The company supplying windshields is having trouble keeping up with orders.

They would ask the fourth why: *Why are they having trouble keeping up?*

Answer: Because there is a shortage of raw materials

The fifth why: *Why is there a shortage of raw materials?*

With this fifth why they have discovered the answer to their original question—Why is windshield installation delayed? Because a shortage of raw materials is slowing the production of windshields.

They could continue to address a symptom by reprimanding or repeatedly replacing the windshield installer, but until they address the supply shortage, they'll never truly address the issue. The same thing is true in our lives. If we continue to treat only the presenting symptoms, we may blame the wrong people or wrong causes over and over without any solution.

Here's an example taken word for word from my journal:

Problem: This week, I have been overwhelmed, short-tempered, and anxious.

Why have I been overwhelmed, short-tempered, and anxious?

Because we have two new employees and I want them to have a good experience on our staff. I always feel like my leadership weaknesses are exposed when someone new joins the team.

*Why does this exposure overwhelm me and stress me
out?*

Because I think our organization should already be a
perfectly well-oiled machine with no possible areas of
improvement.

Why is it important that it be a well-oiled machine?

Because I don't want people to think I am incompetent
or bad at what I do.

Why am I afraid of people thinking I am incompetent?

Because I want to be the best at everything I do.

Why do I need to be the best at this in particular?

Because my identity is tied up in being good at this. If
new employees have a terrible experience, I'm finding
my identity in something I'm bad at.

This fifth question answers my original one. I'm overwhelmed, stressed, and anxious because my identity is tied
up in being a good leader. If these new employees have a bad
experience, this calls my whole identity into question. These
are high stakes for something as mundane as new employee
orientation.

Note: There isn't anything special about the number five.
Sometimes four or six whys can get you to the answer you
need. I usually know I've pressed far enough when it gets
painful to admit to myself what's going on. It's a bit like
hitting a nerve.

Discuss These Scenarios with a Mentor, Counselor, or Pastor

A mentor, counselor, or pastor can help you understand
how to respond differently to these emotions, instinctive ac-

tions, or impulsive reactions in future scenarios. They can also help you address false beliefs, problematic sources of your identity, and untrue messages you tell yourself.

Practice New Habits and Ways of Thinking

If you feel the impulse to jump in and rescue a situation when it's not your responsibility to do so, practice exercising restraint and let others feel the weight of responsibility or even fail. This adjustment will be hard for you and those around you who have become accustomed to you jumping in and making everything okay. The power of this practice is both the freedom it gives you and the sense of responsibility and ownership it requires of those who should have felt these things all along.

I have an extraordinary team member who always executes responsibilities with excellence. However, I fear this way of working will burn him out because of how often it requires him to take responsibility for something someone else on his team is responsible for.

I've continually encouraged this person to be okay with letting things not meet their level of perfection if it means someone on their team will feel the burden of their responsibility. It'll also force others to get creative about solving their problems rather than waiting for him to step in and do it for them. This is hard emotional work in the short term but incredibly liberating and freeing in the long run. This way of working promotes not only their individual mental and emotional health but the health of the team as well.

The need to make everything okay is real. This challenge runs deep in our bones and can't be changed just by being aware of it. Getting to the point where we can let go will take a great deal of work. When we finally do, we will begin to leverage the good baggage packed in this challenge for the good of our relationships. Unfortunately, what trips us up when it comes to making our relationships okay is our uncertainty about what a "normal" relationship is in the first place. It's hard to know how to make things okay when we don't really know what okay looks like.

2

WHAT IS A NORMAL RELATIONSHIP ANYWAY?

As a nine-year-old boy, I remember how strange it was to spend the night at friends' houses and go to bed without the sounds of parents arguing.

Growing up in a family system with addiction meant that when I was with families who didn't have such apparent dysfunction, I became painfully aware that my family wasn't "normal." The truth I didn't know was that I saw friends' families only from the outside. My knowledge was limited to the appearances that all families tend to project.

I concluded that where I came from wasn't normal, and normal families presented the ideal. Given that no family system is perfect, these two choices were both bad models to follow. One was destructive in its dysfunction, the other destructive in its impossible appearance of perfection. This pursuit of perfection would prove doubly harmful given my tendency, as a child of alcoholism, to present the perfect image and to correct all my family's flaws in my own family now.

Part of my journey has been working to live in this imperfection without being disappointed in myself or repeating the mistakes of dysfunction. The issue is that adult children of dysfunctional families often struggle because they have to guess what's normal. The only frame of reference we have is that of a dysfunctional system. It's what we grew up in and all that we know. At some point in our lives, we realized not everyone grew up like we did. That led to us seeing ourselves as different and establishing relationships with the outside world that often feel empty or shallow.

What does this uncertainty about normal look like in our day-to-day lives? It means we look at things that seem to be normal and copy them. It means we're confused about things we believe other people don't get confused about. It means we find ourselves in situations where we don't want to look stupid, so when people make statements like "There are no stupid questions," we think to ourselves, *You don't know my question.*

Survival Roles

Many of us also take on survival roles in response to the relational pain in our lives. Survival roles are adaptations that children unconsciously make to cope in dysfunctional family contexts. These roles also shape how we feel about ourselves and how we conduct ourselves in relationships outside the dysfunctional context.

In their book *After the Tears*, Jane Middelton-Moz and Lorie Dwinell provide an excellent summary of these roles.[1]

Caretaker/Overachiever/Hero

» The caretaker/overachiever/hero struggles with the need to be right and in control and resists feeling dependent on anyone. Those of us in this role are uncomfortable with intimacy. We tend to marry or partner with those who "need" us in some way, and we find ourselves as caretakers in friendships.

» We have difficulty expressing emotions; consequently, our bodies must tell us through physical illness. For this reason, we will endure and demonstrate outstanding leadership, only to be brought down by health issues.

» We beat ourselves up over every mistake we make and may even choose not to do some things if we can't do them perfectly.

Rebel/Scapegoat/Acting-Out Child

» The rebel/scapegoat/acting-out child struggles to take responsibility for their actions. Those of us who fill this role often find ourselves in trouble at school or acting out against coworkers in the workplace. As a result, we struggle to find success and run away from difficulties.

» We may have dropped out of school and/or acted out with rebellious behavior.

» We look for peers with caretaking/codependent tendencies to take care of us but struggle to express gratitude and appreciation for them. Instead, we may return their kindness with cruel or even abusive treatment.

» We tend to act out feelings rather than express them verbally and find expressions of vulnerability or compassion too "soft" for the persona we want to portray.

Adjuster/Withdrawn or Lost Child

» The adjuster/withdrawn or lost child tends to isolate themselves and feels safest when going unnoticed. Those of us who find ourselves in this role shy away from leadership and attention, even playing down our abilities to avoid being noticed.

» We may choose to be withdrawn, even in relationships, and look for those who allow us to remain invisible like we did in our family of origin.

» We struggle with a low sense of self-worth and lack a sense of control over our lives. In this way, we suffer through life with a sense of helplessness.

Pleaser/Clown/Mascot

» The pleaser/clown/mascot copes with the dysfunction of their family life by becoming what others want them to be.

» Those of us who find ourselves in this role struggle to have a sense of our identity because it gets lost in what we think others want us to be.

» We may use humor excessively to escape the tension of difficult situations and to relieve the fear that people aren't taking us seriously anyway.

» Because of our lack of identity, we tend to enmesh ourselves with those we are in a relationship with.

These relationships now define our identity. This also makes it difficult for us to accept that our partners are their own person, separate from us.

» We struggle with setting and keeping boundaries, expressing anger, or stating needs because we fear these will make us unappealing to those around us.

Knowing what was normal was essential to all of us, regardless of our role. It was just important to us for different reasons.

For some of us, normal was a goal to achieve. For others, it was an impression to hide behind. For those of us who filled the role of rebel/scapegoat/acting-out child, we have blamed our family's failure to be normal for all our problems. This, too, informed our identity in its own way.

I personally filled the role of pleaser/clown/mascot. I found the greatest safety in conforming to what I thought others wanted me to be. Knowing what was normal was important to me because if I could conform to normal, I would be okay.

Sources of Normal

Because we didn't know what normal was, many of us from dysfunctional families assumed what we saw on TV was normal. I followed this to such a degree that it bothered me when friends said these TV families weren't real.

They had to be real. They were what I fantasized things could be one day. This possibility was the only thing that got me through some days. I had fantasies such as my dad coming through the door with a bouquet of flowers and a complete change of heart, apologizing to my mom to make it all better. I saw this on TV shows and *dreamed* of it happening at home.

We children of dysfunctional families had no normalcy and stability, so we constructed fantasies to escape the tumult. We imagined what it would be like if our parent showed up for us and got the help they needed or if our parents got back together. We did the same for our future relationships and even our careers. But these fantasies were wholly untethered from reality.

How were we supposed to know? We just thought it was what our relationships could be "if . . ."

Just as we imagined the marriage our parents could have had or the mother or father our parents could have been, we dreamed about what kind of father or mother we would be one day. And then we told ourselves that this idea is what we should be, with no frame of reference for what's normal.

Failing the Fantasy

Now as adults, we constantly blame ourselves when we fail that fantasy from our childhood. Do you question whether your problems are because you haven't worked hard enough, studied hard enough, or prepared enough? Do you second-guess yourself and wonder if you're doing this right? With all your second-guessing, do you undermine your own presence and confidence in relationships?

In our minds, this means we're failing and forfeiting the fantasy. Rather than understanding that our idea was unrealistic, we judge and condemn ourselves mercilessly for failing. It's not that these relationships can't be wonderful and fulfilling. They absolutely can be. But every marriage has its challenges, and every parent is imperfect. It doesn't mean we're with the wrong person or we need to work harder. It means we need to understand that limitations are normal.

We aren't responsible for making it all perfect, just like we weren't responsible for fixing it all when we were kids. The God who got us through then is still getting us through now. When we look at stories in Scripture we see many characters who had to guess what normal was. Consequently, we see a lot of children repeat their parents' mistakes because they didn't know they weren't healthy.

Abraham, Isaac, and Generational Dysfunction

Father Abraham is no exception to the stories of dysfunctional relationships in the Bible. Almost as soon as we meet him, we learn he told a ruler that his wife was his sister to save his own hide. He did this not once but *twice*. In Genesis 12, Abraham asked Sarah to tell Pharoah's men that she was his sister for his own protection. He prioritized his security at the cost of subjecting her to sexual mistreatment. But God came through as the "husband" Abraham wouldn't be and rescued her from this sexual abuse by inflicting Pharoah and his household with disease.

On another occasion, in Genesis 20, Abraham asked her to do the same with King Abimelech. It's no wonder Abraham's son Isaac assumed this must be "normal," given that his father did it twice.

In Genesis 26, a famine drove Isaac into the land of the Philistines and their king, Abimelech. Fearing for his life,

Isaac, too, claimed his wife, Rebekah, was his sister. This time Abimelech discovered the lie when he caught Isaac caressing his wife.

By the third generation, Jacob's family history is full of fathers who lied to save their own skins. As best we know, Jacob never told any pharaohs or kings that his wife was his sister. But he absolutely used deception to sway outcomes in his direction. He swindled his brother out of his birthright, inheritance, and family blessing. The fact that his mother contrived this last con didn't help his proclivity for deception. He even swindled his father-in-law out of the best of his flock (Gen. 30–31). It's no wonder Jacob's name means "trickster."

One of the significant challenges for those of us who grew up in dysfunctional family systems is that we default to the same unhealthy family practices and behaviors, especially in moments of uncertainty, fear, or insecurity. It's tough to think clearly enough to correct unhealthy family habits when a current relationship reenacts a relational dynamic from our childhood. Our heart rate begins to rise, our adrenaline starts to rush, and our thoughts race in pursuit of an escape because we've entered the fight-flight-or-freeze mode.

In the aftermath of one of these episodes where we've unconsciously repeated the actions of our unhealthy family of origin, it can be difficult not to become frustrated with ourselves. We may say, "I'm just like my father" or "I'm just like my mother. I'm never going to change!" This is especially true when parenting our own children.

One night I'd been with all three of our kids all day, and I had reached the end of myself. The kids were constantly picking at one another, arguing and fighting over whose toys were whose and who got to pick the next song in the car, and one child was screaming "Be quiet!" because the other two were being too loud, and on and on. As we were nearing bedtime, I was fed up and then one of my sons lost his mind because his sister had his LEGO. I yelled in my loudest, angriest voice, "AHHH!!! Get in your bed now!!!"

As I saw the look of fear come across his face, my son immediately began to cry and I deflated as I thought to myself, *I'm exactly like my father.*

What was the point of all this work to be different from my father when I acted just like him when it mattered most? In this moment of exasperation, I defaulted to the only thing I knew—producing order and obedience through fear and intimidation. I carry vivid memories of my father's face and voice from the times he responded this way to me when I was a child, and here I was, creating the same vivid memories of my face and voice for my own children.

What was the point in trying?

How We Change

The good news is, we *can* change these reactions, and it's better to work toward this in hopes of producing fewer of these memories for our kids. The bad news is, the process of disarming these reactive triggers isn't a fast one. In fact, it has at least five stages.[2]

Stage 1: Precontemplation

In this stage, we haven't yet acknowledged the negative outcomes of how our childhood has impacted us. We may not be aware that we are reenacting problematic behaviors, or we may be in denial that our family of origin has impacted us. In either case, we haven't yet accepted our present behavior's connection to our past experience.

Stage 2: Contemplation

At this point we are aware of our need to change, but we lack the desire or sense of urgency to do what's necessary to change. We may feel like it's not that serious or that others are making too big a deal of things.

Stage 3: Preparation

By this point we know we want to change and begin developing a plan for change. The problem is, it's difficult to realize in the moment that we're reenacting behaviors from our family of origin. For that reason, this stage entails a lot of *recognizing after the fact* that we've reenacted a behavior we saw as a child.

After losing it on my son and filling him with fear that night, I asked myself some honest questions:

1. *Where have I seen this response before?*
   We don't just come up with our reactions from nowhere. We often repeat reactions we've seen ourselves. In the absence of more creative, thoughtful alternatives, our brain plays out the reactions it has seen and knows.
2. *What made this feel like the right response in the moment?*
3. *What did it feel like as the anger arose?*
4. *How can I see this building sooner?*

5. *What outcome did I hope for and why?*
   In this moment, I wanted peace and quiet. I wanted my children to comply with my commands, and in the absence of other tools, I resorted to the only thing I had, which was my memory of what was used to silence me—anger.

I took my answers to these questions and planned for a better response in the future.

1. I will begin paying attention to what it feels like for my emotions to rise.
2. I will begin to identify the false beliefs that drive my frustration and rash behavior. These include the beliefs that my peace depends on my children's compliance, I'm not a good parent if my kids don't listen, and I'm not a good parent if I don't know what to do at all times and in all situations.
3. I will begin practicing emotional awareness. When I feel the emotion rising, I will stop myself, compose my thoughts, and develop a course of action—even if it means the kids fight a little longer while I figure out the plan.
4. I will begin to resist the pressures I feel from those around me. I will resist the pressure to always have my children in perfect control. I will resist the pressure to be a husband who always knows how to handle things right away. None of these expectations are real or realistic. Even if they are real, they don't contribute to me being the kind of father I want to be.

Stage 4: Action

In Stage 4, we begin implementing our plan of change. Stage 4 may be the most painful stage in the process because we must recognize in the moment that we're reenacting a behavior we don't like. In the absence of newly developed habits, we respond exactly the way we don't want to. At this point we are still developing the capacity to control our emotional response and internalizing the practices we committed to in stage 3. This means we still struggle to alter our course of action in the moment.

It's important not to become discouraged or frustrated. Even the ability to observe ourselves responding in ways we don't like is progress.

Some of our most painful experiences as parents have been watching ourselves reenact events like the episode I described above. In such moments, we've felt the guilt come over us even as we couldn't stop ourselves. But this, too, was a step in the right direction. This time we realized it in the moment. Maybe next time we can identify the anger welling up in us before it reaches the surface.

Stage 5: Maintenance

In stage 5, we are solidifying and reinforcing the changes we made in the action stage. By now we can identify the patterns of behavior and even the emotional buildup in ourselves that lead to the kinds of behavior we want to avoid.

As I identified the patterns and what it felt like for the emotion to rise, I developed the capacity to stop and alter my reaction before it happened. This was transformation. The unhealthy actions I once mistook as instinct were now identified as learned behavior that could be changed. As my counselor often tells me, "Personality cannot change, but behavior can."

We may have even been told by a parent that we *made* them respond a certain way. My father used to tell us that he was going to go to hell because we made him cuss. I once thought I'd really be responsible for that. I now know that no one is responsible for the way we respond except ourselves. You and I are responsible for our own emotions and reactions. If we want to change the cycles of our families, we can begin by owning our emotions and reactions, not casting responsibility for them onto others.

It's Going to Take Time

As you begin working through these stages, you'll identify unhealthy behavior in yourself that you want to end but can't immediately stop. It isn't a light switch. It takes practice. It's important to celebrate the progress of simply identifying the unhealthy behavior. It will be discouraging at times, but remember, this is progress. Be patient with yourself.

Can you imagine if your parent or parents had done this work? Can you imagine if your parent with alcoholism had begun to recognize how problematic their drinking was? If they'd begun a journey to understand what led them to believe alcohol was their only option? If they'd begun to understand the patterns that led to substance use before they used it? If they'd begun to practice new habits that prevented the pattern in the first place?

For many of us, even if it took a couple of years, we would've preferred it over the decades they spent in addiction and self-destruction. We would've preferred it over the brokenness we still live with. If only they could have at least acknowledged the pain they caused, and maybe even apologized.

Change in our relationships that takes time is better than no change at all.

What about Our Lack of Awareness about What's Normal?

To this point, we have taken for granted what it means for a relationship to be "normal." We have worked from the common assumption that normal equates to good, acceptable, appropriate, or even healthy. None of these definitions are true by default. For this reason, I'd like to close this chapter by offering a better criteria by which to judge our relationships: relational healthiness.

No Such Thing as Normal

By "normal," what we usually mean is "perceived as common." But common to whom? What we deem as normal has many influencing factors—economics, race, family size, geographic location, and so on. When we determine a normal, we often become dogmatic about perfecting that ideal and potentially destroy the relationship out of a desire to perfect it.

Pursue Healthy, Not Normal

That's why I encourage you to pursue relational health, not relational normalcy. Healthy means developing important relationship skills like good communication, effective conflict resolution, mutual respect, and healthy boundaries. Focusing on these aspects of a relationship can be more productive for understanding what we've brought with us from our dysfunctional family system. We can then begin the work of dismantling the relationally destructive habits we formed in childhood and replacing them with new ones.

As a parent, not knowing what's normal may cause us to feel immense pressure to be perfect and to have perfect children. I constantly worry I'm repeating mistakes I saw or parenting wrong because I'm unknowingly mimicking something I witnessed that wasn't good or healthy. I also fear I'm simply parenting my children badly because I just don't know any better. The temptation in these moments is to compare my parenting to the parenting of those around me.

I compare myself to how present other fathers are in their preschoolers' lives or how other parents respond to their children when they're disobedient. But this isn't necessarily an indication of health and entails making assumptions about the mental and emotional well-being of other parents.

In choosing to pursue health over normalcy, I began to consider what it looks like to assess my parenting using more objective measures: How able am I to regulate my emotions? When I grow frustrated with my children, do I discipline as consistently as I can? Do I discipline with composure or with anger and outbursts? Do I strike a healthy balance between work and family? Do I have good boundaries that enable me to be present with my kids? Do I support my wife well? Do I work alongside her as both a healthy spouse and a healthy model for my sons?

These questions proved to be better objective parameters and helped protect me from the subjectivity and insecurity of comparing myself to other parents.

Pursuing Normal Can Become a Prison

A few years ago, I noticed a pattern of behavior when I started new jobs. I would go through orientation without asking any questions and then I'd begin work and find myself completely lost. I refused to ask questions because I feared appearing incompetent, or I assumed it was something I should already know. I was also afraid of upsetting someone by asking stupid questions. As a result, I'd find myself in the frustrating situation of having to figure things out for myself.

This changed during a review of a new benefits plan at work. I had lots of questions about the plan but felt it was inappropriate to ask them, again because "I should just know these things." However, as soon as someone else began asking many of the same questions I had, I realized I wasn't the only one who didn't know these things.

It sounds silly to say, but it was profoundly freeing to simply ask and get the answers I needed. I began to accept that it was better to risk appearing incompetent to get the answers I needed than to preserve my pride and struggle on my own. Not being concerned about appearing incompetent provided a certain freedom.

I also realized that most people wouldn't respond in anger just because I had a few clarifying questions. I wasn't intruding on their time or disappointing them by asking about something they were training me on. That's why I needed *training*. In fact, in a healthy work environment, people prefer that I ask questions to produce the right results the first time.

The hardest part about not knowing what's normal is not having any frame of reference for when we've arrived at normal. That's why healthy is a better objective. Regardless of our starting point or childhood environment, what we all want is relational health.

Some of us may have had a head start because we were formed in a context that modeled relational health. But where we started doesn't determine where we end up. Experiencing bad relationships in our childhood doesn't predestine us to be bad at relationships for life.

3

CAN ANYTHING GOOD COME FROM WHAT I'VE BEEN THROUGH?

There's nothing a child of difficult circumstances wants more than healthy relationships of their own.

Having experienced the brokenness of my parents' marriage, I knew that above and beyond anything else, what I desired most for my own marriage was a healthy, flourishing, life-giving relationship. Some of this may have come from my need to prove I was a different kind of father and husband than my own father had been. But even more than that, I had experienced the pain of broken parental relationships first-hand and didn't want to inflict the same pain on my children.

Within the first year of our marriage, Sharon and I made a commitment to meet with a counselor monthly. We've done so now for twelve years, and it's become one of the most foundational practices of our marriage. This commitment to meeting with a counselor on a regular basis—regardless of whether we feel we need it or not—has protected us in some crucial ways. It prevented us from ever having to ask, "Has this gotten bad enough that we need to talk to someone about it?" It also allowed us to deal with problems while they were still small. And so, as we like to say, we go to a counselor not because we have big problems, but because we don't want big problems.

I've also seen that in many struggling relationships, counseling is a last-ditch effort to save the relationship—or worse, couples attend counseling to present the appearance of having "tried everything." But often by this point, one or both spouses already have a foot out the door. The level of love required to do the necessary selfless work to heal the relationship is already gone. Counseling can simply become a hoop to jump through on the way to divorce rather than something you're pursuing because you want to see the relationship repaired.

We share this practice openly to create a safe environment for others to understand the importance of counseling. I include the following in my charge to every couple I marry: "Plans fail for lack of counsel, but with many advisers they succeed" (Prov. 15:22 NIV). This is no less true for the marriage relationship.

However, I'm not naive to the stigma that therapy and counseling still have, especially among Christians. There have certainly been times when people have been a bit scandalized by our counseling and wondered if we're "okay." But the truth of the matter is, I've seen the cost of not pursuing health in a marriage relationship. Our going to counseling means we have very few priorities above pursuing the health of our marriage.

The Drive to Do Better

Our experiences with broken relationships when we were children produced a relentless drive in us as adults to pursue healthy relationships of our own. This is the good baggage that underlies everything else our childhood did to prepare us for exceptional relationships. This drive enables us to overcome many of the obstacles to healthy relationships that can readily derail the work of relational healing.

Why does a difficult childhood produce this drive? I've got three reasons.

Pain and Motivation

First, our difficult childhood produced this drive because pain is a powerful motivator. As children who grew up in difficult circumstances and experienced the deep pain of watching a marriage fall apart, many of us made commitments to ourselves to never experience that kind of pain in our own relationships.

As an elementary-age child, I remember many nights hearing my parents fight while I went to sleep and many nights wishing they'd just separate. I vividly remember the night they ultimately did. We all went over to my dad's new place, and my siblings and I sat in in the back of our brown Ford minivan as my parents talked outside. I cried and thought to myself, *What have I done? Why did I wish this on them?*

In hindsight I can see clearly this wasn't something I caused. It wasn't my fault in any way. However, as children, we're unable to make such distinctions, especially when we already feel responsible for others' feelings and actions.

The layers of pain inflicted were tremendous, including the pain of watching my parents' relationship break down and the pain I experienced carrying guilt about what had happened. As I grew up, I reaffirmed that commitment to myself to never experience or cause that kind of pain in my own marriage and family. In this way, pain has proven to be a powerful motivator.

What We Didn't Have

Second, our difficult childhood produced a drive to fulfill what we ourselves didn't have in our parents. This step goes beyond pain and overcorrection to positively articulate a vision for what we want relationally.

When I was a high school student, my community had a gathering that regularly addressed drug and alcohol use. I was often invited to share about my experience as a child of a parent with alcoholism. A distinct element of the story I always shared was the pain I experienced in feeling as though my father had chosen alcohol over a relationship with me. I'd express how painful it was that having a relationship with me and his love for me weren't enough to motivate him to get the help he needed.

In hindsight I understand now how much more complicated addiction is. This, however, is a crucial element of the pain inflicted on adult children of dysfunctional families—we can't process others' decisions separately from their reflection on us. Thus, we internalize the negative message of their actions as a message about us.

I vowed to myself then that I'd never allow my own pride to get in the way of having healthy relationships with my spouse or my children. As a husband and father who has now experienced my own struggle with substances, I reaffirm that commitment to healing for the sake of my wife and children to fulfill what I didn't have. The vision I have for these relationships is a powerful motivator to do things differently.

A Clear Vision of What We Don't Want

Third, we have a very clear picture of what we *don't* want for our relationships. We're driven by the desire not to be what we saw. In my dating relationships, I was driven to be attentive to the needs of my girlfriends, to be self-sacrificing, to place their needs above my own, to be aware of their feelings, to be sensitive, and to be willing to listen. And in no circumstances was it ever acceptable to be angry or express negative emotions.

But knowing what not to do didn't equal knowing what to do. In many relationships I was driven more by what I knew not to be more than who I was supposed to be. The crucial element to understand is this: we have an unrelenting drive for healthy relationships because we know where relationships go when they go badly.

A major blind spot occurs when we pursue relationships but aren't yet healthy ourselves. In such instances, we may neglect our own feelings, desires, and thoughts to do what's necessary to keep our partner happy. This may not be healthy, but the outcome sure seems healthier than what we saw growing up.

The fact of the matter is, we may want healthy relationships, but if we haven't first done the work to restore our own mental and emotional health, no relationship will be enough to fix this for us. But when we're able to access the right tools and do the right kind of work, we will be set up for truly healthy relationships.

How Did Our Childhood Prepare Us for Healthy Relationships?

As I examined my own experiences and assessed my approach to having relationships different from the ones I witnessed growing up, I learned that it was key to set the right priorities.

Humility

First, our drive for healthier relationships enables us to prioritize humility. One of the greatest obstacles to relational healing and strength is pride. Pride is an obstacle to vulnerability and therefore to intimacy in relationships. It produces self-defensiveness, and defensiveness is an obstacle to owning mistakes and wrongdoing. This, in turn, becomes an obstacle to effective communication and conflict resolution.

However, when we're willing to own the brokenness we've caused, it becomes a powerful use of humility for the good of the relationship. This willingness to take responsibility for our mistakes may not come easily, but the desire to be focused on others and have a different kind of relationship may soften this resistance.

Relationally speaking, resolution can't begin until disarming and de-escalation have taken place. We lower the temperature of an argument when one of us is willing to be the first to put down our arms, listen to the other, and show understanding as a demonstration of care for the relationship, not just what's at stake for us individually.

Early in our marriage, when Sharon and I argued, the typical cycle began with some discussion that I inevitably became defensive about. Sharon, being quick-witted and a master wordsmith, would unload her argument on me like a machine gun firing off its rounds—*budududududu*. I would then shut down, and Sharon would retreat to the bedroom to "reload."

She would emerge, the argument would resume, and the cycle would continue until one of us finally stopped arguing and started listening. We demonstrated our listening by rehearsing what we heard the other saying. "So, what I hear you saying is . . ." became the phrase that indicated one of us was tired of arguing and wanted to move the discussion in a more productive direction.

But this also forfeited our ground to "win" the argument. We had to care more about the relationship than winning, and that often meant acknowledging the legitimate hurt the other person had felt.

Humility is the key that unlocks this ability to acknowledge the brokenness we've caused or the wrong we've done. This doesn't mean we take responsibility for things we didn't cause or do. It means we're willing to take the first step to disarm and de-escalate the direction of the argument because we care more about the relationship than "winning."

Long-Term Gain Is Worth Short-Term Pain

This leads to the second way in which our difficult childhood prepared us for healthy relationships: it taught us to value long-term gain over avoiding short-term pain. In other words, we have *grit*. We realize that the short-term pain necessary to heal a relationship is far better than the pain of long-term brokenness. Often the short-term pain is the humiliation involved in admitting everything isn't okay and asking for help. The consequence of avoiding this short-term pain is perpetuating the ongoing, compounding impact of the unhealth we didn't ask for or deserve but nevertheless inherited as children.

When I share with others that Sharon and I go to counseling, one of the common responses we get is "But isn't that expensive? How do you afford it?" My response is a little tongue-in-cheek, but I reply, "Have you ever seen a divorce? We can't afford not to!" The reality is, it's either an expense we pay on the front end for health and happiness in our relationship, or it's a lump sum of cash we pay at the end—on top of pain, brokenness, despair, and grief of a lost relationship. The long-term gain is worth the short-term pain.

As a child who grew up in difficult circumstances, we were often aware of what the long-term gain could be, if only our parent or parents would do the work necessary to bring the healing. Though we didn't see healing realized, this experience ingrained in us what should be done and should be valued for the good of the relationship.

While my parents were separated, my father was diagnosed with prostate cancer. My mom saw this as a second chance for their relationship and for their marriage. After my father's surgery to remove the cancer, he moved back home and things seemed to be heading in the right direction. But it wasn't long before my father returned to using alcohol, eventually leading to their final separation and divorce.

I often wonder what might've been if my father had really committed himself to healing. *What if he had been able to see the long-term gain of the short-term pain to address his addiction? How would things have been different? Would he still be alive because he chose to stop drinking at that point? Could my parents still be together? Could his healing have been a powerful witness to the healing that God can bring* to a relationship? Could it have been a witness to the way tragedies can lead to beautiful things?

Fighting for One Another

Finally, our difficult childhood prepared us for healthy relationships in that it taught us the importance of fighting for one another. The beauty of this is, when we learn to fight for each other, we find that we don't have to fight for ourselves. We don't have to fight for our needs because we know the other person is already doing that for us.

This is a profoundly biblical picture of what God invites us into as his people. When the apostle Paul instructs us to carry one another's burdens, to bear with one another in love, to see ourselves as one body with many parts, we're fighting for one another. When one member of the body suffers, the whole body suffers. Conversely, this means that when we fight against one another, we're fighting against ourselves. God doesn't permit us to see ourselves in such individualistic terms (Rom. 12:3–9; 15:1–3; 1 Cor. 12; Gal. 6:2; Eph. 4:1–2). In a loving, self-sacrificing relationship, we fight *for* one another. This is a beautiful and biblical image of a healthy relationship.

You may struggle to ever feel like things are okay. You may feel unequipped for "normal" relationships. But I also believe you have the same passion for relational health that I've described here. It's why you're reading this book.

You may feel like you don't have the know-how, experience, or tool kit to have the kind of relationships you want, but that's what this book is for. Together we're going to take the passion and good baggage our difficult childhood put in us and learn how to leverage them for the good of our relationships now.

PT 2 | THE CYCLE SABOTAGING OUR RELATIONSHIPS

Addressing the cycle of sabotage is a crucial first step to realizing the kind of relationships we've always wanted. This cycle operates on a level so far below the surface that many of us feel the struggle but can't name it. We can't name it because the dysfunction of our childhood produced coping mechanisms that operate without our awareness.

The hard part is, these coping mechanisms served a purpose for a long time. They served us well until they didn't. Now we must do some interior examination to understand how our relational system operates and why it's now working against us.

We'll begin with codependency because it's the gateway to the rest of the cycle. The people-pleasing and loss of self that characterize codependency drive the approval-seeking that follows. Once we understand codependency, we'll understand why we burn out on people-pleasing and fall into deception as a means of self-protection, and why codependency keeps us from enforcing the boundaries we so desperately need.

4

CODEPENDENCY

I'll Be Whoever You Want Me to Be

At the age of nineteen, I was barely older than the students I'd been hired to serve in my first ministry position. The parents of these students could've been my own parents and so, quite naturally, I began to interact with them as such. I was devastated when I didn't meet their expectations and elated when I exceeded them. In short, my value rose and fell with whether they approved of me.

This was particularly true with the dads. In hindsight, it's clear this was due to the complicated relationship I had with my own dad. The fear I had of my dad transferred to a fear of them, as did my desire to gain their approval and ensure they were always happy with me. The same complicated feelings I'd had with my father, I now felt toward them—but with no awareness of why.

I was constantly assessing my standing with them. I found myself covertly deducing an approval rating or pandering for compliments and feedback. The impact of the problems in my family of origin was wreaking havoc in these relationships. I was desperate to gain their approval, and I molded myself in this role to manipulate that approval from them.

This is one of the more significant challenges in addressing the ongoing impact of a difficult childhood—we transfer our complicated feelings about those from early in our lives onto those in our lives now.

In this chapter, we'll identify exactly how our childhood causes us to manipulate others for approval. The heart of this chapter is to identify the cause of this people-pleasing in our past to remove it from our future.

The Power and Problem of Codependency

In my own context, codependency was the relational consequence of constantly accommodating and appeasing the unpredictability of my father's alcoholism.

In *Emotional Sobriety*, Tian Dayton says, "Codependency is a trauma-related loss of self."[1] We experience a loss of self because living alongside a substance-dependent or unhealthy person leaves us with no sense of who we are apart from their needs and approval.[2] In codependency, our lives become entirely enmeshed with someone else's, either out of a need for survival or as a means of emotional stability. The central idea of codependency is "Who do you want me to be?"

Dayton also explains that codependency is fear-based. This is due not only to the literal danger we lived in, but also because we now associate disapproval with unjust punishment. For those of us who grew up in an abusive environment specifically, disapproval regularly included a severe dressing-down complete with insults, condescension, blame, and even physical beatings. As a result, disapproval wasn't just someone's logical disagreement with our action or performance. Disapproval meant judgment, and the punishment rarely fit the crime (if a "crime" had even been committed). Disapproval now triggers us to brace for impact. We fear everyone's disapproval will be as abusive as the dysfunctional individual in our lives.

Codependency and My Identity

My codependency was in high gear as Sharon and I led Bright City through the pandemic, racial tensions, and political polarization of 2020. As I've shared, the emotional exhaustion of this season led me to misuse my medication. At that point I took a month off and during this time away, I read Melody Beattie's *Codependent No More*. Beattie pinpoints that a core characteristic of codependency is feeling responsible for the feelings and actions of those around you. You feel a responsibility to manage others' feelings and reactions.

Up until this point in my life, I truly believed that if someone was upset with me, I could work it out through a conversation and get us back to a healthy place. However, during this season in which I was the target of many people's anger and had experienced failure after failure to restore these relationships through conversation and "good behavior," I was exasperated. I couldn't just "fix" people's feelings and emotions. The unresolved disapproval was crushing.

You'd think I would have been happy to see these people go, but in typical codependent fashion, I couldn't let them go. I couldn't let them go because I didn't know who I was apart from their approval. I couldn't let them go because their leaving was a referendum on my performance; their leaving meant I was a failure. I needed them, even if it was painful, because I couldn't define my sense of purpose apart from the sacrifices I made to meet their needs. In other words, as much as I hated the pain it caused me, I functioned as if I was addicted to them.

How Codependency Is an Obstacle to Healthy Relationships

This kind of codependency becomes an obstacle to healthy relationships for at least three reasons:

1. It's impossible to have healthy relationships when you can't distinguish your own identity from who you think others want you to be.
2. It's impossible to have healthy relationships when you aren't confident enough to differentiate yourself from others in a relationship.
3. It's impossible to have a healthy relationship when, at a base level, you don't know who you are.

Obstacle 1: Who You Are versus Who Others Want You to Be

In our efforts at emotional and physical self-protection as children, we worked to become whatever we thought we needed to be to ensure our parents embraced us. Who did we need to be to avoid rejection, the silent treatment, abandonment, or abuse? This was how we established a sense of peace and stability. However, this prevented us from developing a sense of our own identity. Because we lacked our own identity we opted instead to be what everyone around us wanted us to be.

As a child, I became a kind of chameleon who could move fluidly between identities. Growing up, we lived on a farm, rented several pastures, and had all manner of livestock, from cattle and horses to chickens, goats, and even a couple of emus at one point. In other words, I grew up a bit of a country boy, complete with Wrangler jeans, cowboy boots, and belt buckles.

However, my country-boy life was foreign to my friends at school. The elementary school I attended was close to Chapel Hill, North Carolina, which was a much more suburban and progressive area.

I'd often morph into a different version of myself around my school friends. I was a country cowboy on the weekends and a soccer-playing, preppy kid during the week. For me, changing identities was as simple as changing clothes. In third grade, a friend from school invited me to attend a rodeo. I remember being completely stressed out about what to wear because so much of my morphing identities had to do with the clothes I wore. On the one hand, this was a rodeo, where it was completely acceptable to be myself—a Wrangler jeans–wearing cowboy in boots, a belt buckle, and a cowboy hat. On the other hand, I'd never seen, much less imagined, my Chapel Hill friend donning Western attire. This moment couldn't have been more perfectly orchestrated to bring my lack of identity into sharp relief.

I opted to play it safe and dress as I always did for school: high-top Reebok pumps, a pair of black cargo pants with the legs rolled up, and a yellow T-shirt. I was too cool for school. But when my friend and his family arrived, I was mortified to see them come to the door in Wrangler jeans, cowboy boots, and belt buckles.

I was completely humiliated, not only because of my outfit, but because I had been exposed for the fraud I knew I was. To this day, this remains one of the most embarrassing moments in my life. If I'd just been who I most naturally was, I would've been fine.

Out of fear of disappointing my friend, I'd morphed into what I thought he wanted me to be. The pain of that moment sticks with me because even though I didn't know who I was, I had a 50/50 chance of getting it right, and I still chose wrong. As embarrassing as my outfit was, it was nothing compared to the pain of knowing I wasn't content to be myself.

This goes deeper than clothes. When we've been only what those around us want us to be, we've actually shared very little of ourselves. We've communicated only what we thought others wanted from us anyway. This has very little, if anything, to do with them knowing us and much more to do with us aiming to meet their expectations of us.

The consequence of this, ultimately, is a lack of intimacy in our relationships. Intimacy comes from connecting with an authentic self. But if we do not know who we are, we have no authentic self to offer. We have no authentic self to be vulnerable with, much less to trust others to accept.

Unfortunately, we may not even be aware of our lack of intimacy because it's never been something that was a part of our lives. We could either be what others wanted us to be or open ourselves to be known and to know others. But we couldn't be both. Because it was safer to be what others wanted us to be, we closed ourselves off to intimacy.[3]

Many of the difficult circumstances we grew up in exacerbated our inclination to close ourselves off to being known. When we did open ourselves up and were vulnerable, at best those needs went unmet. At worst, our vulnerability was used against us, to hurt us and to ridicule us. In response, we decided it was better to go without expressing those needs than to open ourselves again to potential harm. So we closed ourselves off to the need of intimacy.[4]

In the long run, this undermined our ability to have healthy relationships because healthy relationships require a level of reciprocity. In a healthy relationship, we not only create safe space for others to be vulnerable, but we ourselves are also willing to be vulnerable. When we can't separate our identity from who others want us to be, it's impossible to identify our individual needs, much less communicate those needs to someone else.

When it comes to our needs, this is something we rarely give much thought to. We assume needs present themselves in an objective and undeniable way. But because we've pushed our needs down and away for so long, we've lost sensitivity to them and how they are felt.

When these needs are finally expressed, it's often in unhealthy ways. The pressure of repressed feelings always forces them to the surface in some way. This ultimately destroys the reciprocity of the relationship because the needs are expressed not as relational needs but as relational demands.

Obstacle 2: Differentiation

Codependency also becomes an obstacle in our relationships because we aren't confident enough in ourselves to be a well-differentiated person. We struggle to distinguish between where we end and others begin. In his book *A Failure of Nerve*, Edwin H. Friedman defines a well-differentiated person as "someone who has clarity about his or her own life goals and, therefore, someone who is less likely to become lost in the anxious emotional processes swirling about."[5] The well-differentiated person "can be separate while still remaining connected, and therefore, can maintain a modifying, non-anxious, and sometimes challenging presence."[6]

Most relevant to our work here, the well-differentiated person "can manage his or her own reactivity in response to the automatic reactivity of others, and therefore, be able to take stands at the risk of displeasing."[7]

Using verbal and sometimes physical abuse, my dad transgressed healthy emotional and physical boundaries with everyone in our family. Because I didn't see healthy boundaries demonstrated as a child, it's been difficult now to know where the boundaries fall between me and others.

In particular, it's difficult to know how much of another's feelings, emotions, and actions I'm responsible for. I assume far too much responsibility for others' feelings and actions, especially when they're negative. I'm convinced I've made them feel this way, so I believe it's my responsibility to fix their feelings and reactions, regardless of how rational or irrational, appropriate or inappropriate their responses may be.

In this way, I have become enmeshed with others. I have struggled to distinguish emotionally between what's mine and what's others'. In much the same way that I "managed" the feelings and actions of my father, I attempt to "control" those who are upset with me, and it's exhausting. But I can't stop, because at the end of the day, I am unable to distinguish how others feel about me from how I feel about myself.

A well-differentiated person, however, can remain relationally close to another person without being emotionally hijacked by them. This means we have a clear awareness of what we are and aren't responsible for and can remain in relationship without taking on what's not ours to fix.

In fact, a "fixing" mindset further damages the relationship because it communicates that they can count on us to play that role in the future. Ultimately, they'll come to believe we're responsible for their emotions as well. This becomes an unhealthy, abusive relationship, much like the one in our family of origin.

"Emotional processes" are the ways our brain processes and manages emotions. In our family of origin, we adapted our emotional processes to the emotional processes of the individual or individuals who were creating dysfunction in the first place. This was a subconscious, self-protective mechanism. For example, I processed my dad's anger as a threat and learned to respond with acquiescence. I processed my mom's sadness as my problem to fix and responded with heroism.

Now, long after leaving my childhood context, when someone is angry, my reaction is to disappear. When someone is sad, my reaction is to console.

These malformed emotional processes worked in conjunction with our lack of clear emotional boundaries to perpetuate unhealthy relationships. In these unhealthy relationships, we became the consoler, the fixer, and the rescuer rather than identifying where we end and another begins. This would've required the other party in the relationship to take responsibility for themselves. As children, however, this was impossible to ask of anyone because we'd learned it was dangerous or disastrous to enforce our own boundaries.

We also see this mindset play out in our inability to say no to others. We're unable to say no because we genuinely believe we're responsible for the emotions and reactions of others. We believe that saying no will cause anger. This triggers our fear of the punishment we'll receive for having caused that anger. Or we believe saying no will cause disappointment, which equates to *us being a disappointment*. We feel this even if what has been asked of us is completely inappropriate or simply not possible.

This can be anything, from our boss asking us to work an excessive number of hours to simply saying no to a friend's invitation because we already have something on our calendar. In our codependency, we can't say no because we don't want to upset them. In the moments when we do have to say no, we carry a great deal of guilt. We rarely say no because of our own boundaries or self-respect. More often it's only because two external pressures are at odds with each other.

In the end, we're at war in ourselves. We hate our inability to say no. And yet, in the moment, we cave again because we would rather say yes than carry the weight of guilt that comes from causing someone to react negatively. We'd rather carry frustration with ourselves than guilt from upsetting someone else.

Obstacle 3: Know Who You Are

Finally, this people-pleasing interdependency becomes an obstacle to healthy relationships because it's impossible to have healthy relationships when we don't know ourselves. We've touched on this a bit with the previous two obstacles, but the reason we can't distinguish who we are from what others want us to be or differentiate ourselves from the feelings and reactions of others is this most basic reality: we don't know ourselves. This is due in part to the fact that we've operated as a chameleon for most of our lives. We've shifted identities to fit different environments for so long that it's difficult to know who we really are.

Was I a cowboy or a soccer-playing preppy kid? We've taken on so many identities and pursued so much achievement, recognition, and status to impress or gain approval or become something important. But we've never stopped to ask, "Is this really me?" We've gotten so caught up in who we believe we're supposed to be or what we think will give us value and significance that we've never questioned, "Is this who I am? Is this life-giving to me? Is this what I want to do? Am I trying to fit a mold of what I've been told to be? Can I identify who I am in distinction from these voices?"

When we don't know ourselves, our relationship will ultimately become dysfunctional. This happens because the other person never truly interacts with us—only the facade we present of ourselves. This means there will always be some level of distance between us. However, that distance isn't really between us and them; it's between us and the self we're projecting.

Fight Your Battles the Way *You* Fight Battles

The biblical character King David provides an extraordinary example of how to fight a battle. When young David stepped up to take on the giant Goliath, King Saul put his own armor on him—armor that was much too big. In this moment, it would've been easy to see how David might've thought, *Well, it's too big, but I guess this is how everyone fights their battles. Plus, these guys sure have been doing this a lot longer than I have, so even if it doesn't fit, I'm going to look ridiculous going out to fight Goliath without it!*

However, David had a clear sense of who he was. Therefore, he was able to communicate with confidence that this armor wasn't "him," that it didn't fit him. It didn't fit him literally in size, or figuratively in how he best fought his battles. David didn't cave to the pressure to present himself as someone he wasn't. He also didn't fight with a sword and a shield. David instead fought with a sling and a stone.

The truth is, if David would have kept this armor on, it would've been disastrous. The armor wasn't only too big, it was also unfamiliar to him. Putting on the armor simply to satisfy others would've been to his detriment and to the detriment of others. Ultimately, it would have led to his defeat.

It would've been his downfall because there was a literal (and figurative) distance between him and his armor. There was a distance between who others thought he should be and who he really was. And because he could take off that armor and remove the distance, he was able to be himself. He was able to fight the way he fought battles and ultimately defeated Goliath. Not because he conformed to others' ideas of who he should be but because he knew his true self.[8]

Until we're able to be our true selves, even in the face of disapproval, opposition, and misunderstanding, it's going to be difficult for us to have healthy relationships or find contentment in ourselves. We'll always be focused on who we aren't or what we aren't rather than embracing who we are and the unique strengths that gives us.

We've believed for so long that if enough people are happy with us, we will finally be happy with ourselves. We want contentment, and we believe this comes from the adoration of others. But we need to understand the root causes of this false belief. That's what we'll tackle next as we lay out how codependency and our desperation for approval go hand in hand.

5

APPROVAL SEEKING

If You Love Me, You Won't Hurt Me

Fifteen years ago, my mom built a house tucked into an idyllic corner of her parents' homestead. Because I was still in graduate school and moving around, most of my childhood belongings moved into her attic. Fast-forward fifteen years, and my kids were now snooping around her attic for evidence of my earlier life. Amid their investigation, they stumbled on a large trophy with my name and the title of the award etched into the nameplate: "Male Scholar Athlete of the Year." That year, I also served as a captain on the soccer team and just so happened to be voted homecoming king.

It was quite a year and a real moment of proving to my kids, "See, Dad was cool once." But as I reflected on these accomplishments in light of everything I'd been learning about adult children of dysfunctional families, I began to see it all in a very different way.

In his book *Healing the Child Within*, Charles Whitfield explains how we, as adult children of dysfunctional families, construct identities we believe will be most appealing to others. He describes these as our "false selves." We construct them because the true self or the "inner child" feels that it's rejected or not acceptable or approved of. Therefore, the "true self" should remain hidden to protect us from the pain of exposure, worthlessness, and inadequacy.[1]

How much of my achievement had really been driven by these internal and subconscious motivators? Motivators that I had no way of detecting as a seventeen-year-old boy? How much of this had been an attempt to conceal and protect my inner child from disapproval?

The Cycle Continues

If codependency is a loss of the self, then approval seeking is how we strive to create an identity for ourselves that we believe others will value. We may have been stripped of our internal sense of worth, but maybe, just maybe, we can erect an identity others will approve of.

The problem with the pursuit of value is that at the end of the day, no amount of external approval can make up for an inherent sense of value or the ability to affirm ourselves. That's because we live by this formula: *Self-worth = My Performance + Others' Opinions*.[2]

This is more than image management or self-esteem. It's coping with an unformed ability to affirm ourselves. The lack of a consistent message of affirmation as children deprived us of an internal capacity to validate ourselves, so we constantly seek external sources to do it for us. We live by the lie that we need certain people to approve of us to feel good about ourselves.

When we were children, approval was inconsistent and conditional at best. We now find ourselves crushed by a similar inconsistency and conditionality in seeking the approval of our friends, coworkers, professional societies, community organizations, congregations, and social media followers.

There were moments of affirmation from our parents, either in their substance-induced euphoria or their pride at our overachieving, but it was unpredictable and often disingenuous. Did they mean it or was it the alcohol talking? Were they proud of me or just what my success afforded them? This kind of response to affirmation is now our default. We always question their sincerity. Do they mean it?

It's the reason for our strange paradox: *as much as we yearn for approval, it's difficult to accept when we get it.* Because we received many mixed messages as children—"yes," "no," "I love you," "go away"—we might say, "Well, I have their approval now, but will it be gone tomorrow? What must I do to keep it?" We are fearful that approval is hanging on by a thread and the slightest misstep will sever it.

This is devastating now because we impose the same uncertainty of where we stand onto the people in our lives today. How will people receive me today? Are they happy with me? What did that look mean? Have I done enough lately to ensure embrace and not abuse?

Tools

Below are a few tools that have been helpful for me.

1. *Identify your anxiety zones.* These are all the areas where you are most concerned about receiving the approval and

affirmation of others. You'll experience the most anxiety around the things you seek the most affirmation about.

Once we're able to name these, we can do the five whys exercise from chapter 1 to understand why our performance in these areas is so important. Once we know why, we can begin to change the way we think. We can choose to remove those areas from our lives, limit our engagement, or move them to the realm of enthusiasm, which we will discuss in the next section.

2. *Set performance boundaries.* Because we lack an internal capacity to affirm ourselves, we struggle to know when we've done well enough. We'll overwork to obtain approval, but without boundaries on how far we'll go for approval, we'll become workaholics.

Regarding work, ask for specific targets, goals, or outcomes. With a spouse, ask them to state their expectations of you explicitly. As a parent, seek out professional advice to give you a sense of what's healthy. As long as the conversation stays in your head, there will be no limit to the expectations you place on yourself.

3. *Accept that some people's approval cannot be won.* One of the greatest challenges for us can be accepting that some people's approval simply can't be won. No matter what we do or how hard we try, their approval can't be won because it's not about us in the first place. When we can come to a place of accepting this, the freedom is simply incredible. How much energy and emotional bandwidth could we save if we didn't spend it on people who can't be won?

A step beyond that is finding a level of comfort in yourself that allows you to say, "Who I am is enough. If they can't receive me as I am, that's their problem, not mine." This isn't

intended to sound harsh. (And if this is already your disposi-
tion, I may not be talking to you. You may need to be a little
more open to what others need you to be.) But for those of
us who have spent our lives trying to be what we thought
everyone around us wanted us to be, this is a lifeline that
gives us permission not to be what everyone wants us to be.

4. *Decide that some people's approval isn't worth winning.*
Another thought that may never have crossed our minds is
that there are some people who, even if we could win their
approval, are not worth giving our time and energy to. They
demonstrate many of the same boundary-breaking habits
as those from our childhood.

We can only gain some people's approval by becoming
someone other than ourselves. We must espouse values and
beliefs we don't really have or hold. In such instances, these
people are approving not of us but of a version of us that
conforms to their preferences. It's not worth becoming someone else to gain the approval of someone who has no interest
in who we actually are anyway.

5. Replace *Self-Worth = My Performance + Others' Opinions* with a more biblical formula: *Self-Worth = God's Truth
about You.*

This isn't a mushy "Jesus loves you" mantra. This is the
gospel declaration that God pursued your affection at the
cost of his own life. We don't have to please others to be approved; we already are. We're approved, not because of our
performance but because of his. "God's truth about you is
that you are deeply loved, completely forgiven, fully pleasing, totally accepted, and absolutely complete in Christ."[3]

It's been healing in this area to embrace that who I am
is who God wanted me to be—not just the potential that I

carry, but the specific abilities, gifts, and passions I possess. Even the baggage I have can be redeemed for my good and the healing of others around me.

The Realm of Enthusiasm

At the same time, the things we pursue achievement in, we often enjoy and find life-giving. But because achievement promises significance, many of us have wrung ourselves out on things we love to do in pursuit of that significance. In such moments, the temptation is to drop what we're passionate about because we keep making it about the exhausting work of pursuing recognition and accomplishment. We keep making it about us. Robert Wicks writes,

> Those of us who have tried to compete with the world, doing impressive things as a way of trying to overcome our feelings of inadequacy should continue to try accomplishing things in the world. Yet such accomplishments should not be exhibitionistic or competitive, but should lie in the realm of enthusiasm.[4]

The "realm of enthusiasm" is where we do things because we love to do them, because we were uniquely created to do them, and because it benefits those around us when we do them. We pursue work and activity that we love not because the achievement will give us a sense of value, but because a part of our flourishing is participating in the things we're good at and enthusiastic about. We also find that as we lean into the things we're passionate about, the very act of doing them is satisfying, fulfilling, and meaningful in itself.

When we move our pursuit of achievement into the realm of enthusiasm, we're free to engage these activities simply for the joy of doing them, not for something they'll do for us.

Codependency, Approval Seeking, and Deception

The codependency that many of us brought out of our childhood often leads to the pursuit of approval we have addressed here. But when this pursuit of approval also goes unaddressed, we can unintentionally and even unknowingly slide into using deception as a means of gaining the approval we are so desperate for. As we dive deep into deception in the next chapter, we'll come to see how codependency, approval seeking, and deception work together to sabotage our relationships and what steps we can take to reverse them.

6

DECEPTION

Lying for Love

A few years ago, I made the decision that I wouldn't consume any more alcohol. I made this commitment to Sharon for the sake of our marriage, and given my family history, drinking alcohol just wasn't a good idea anyway.

Not long after making this decision, I went to visit some friends in Chicago. During our time together, we hit one of my favorite spots, a brewpub called the "Lucky Monk." I'd grown to love this brewery and its beautiful golden-brown beer, so quite naturally, I felt a tension between enjoying some of my favorite beverages and remaining true to my commitment.

I knew this would be the only time for a long time to have any of this beer, so I decided to get one of my favorites and only drink a little bit of it. Later that night, when I was talking to Sharon on the phone, she happened to ask if I'd gotten anything to drink. Reflexively, I said, "No."

But as soon as I said it, I not only recognized my lie but was also struck by how instinctively I had lied. I quickly changed my answer and told her that I'd gotten one of my favorite drinks, but this only caused a compounding negative effect on our conversation. On one level, I'd broken what I'd committed to. And on a second level, I'd been dishonest about it.

I'd defaulted so quickly to a dishonest reply because of how deeply ingrained it was in me to lie as a means of avoiding severe punishment. As a child of a parent with alcoholism, I remember how uncertain and unpredictable my father's replies could be to my bad behavior or perceived bad behavior. And so dishonesty became an effective way to avoid punishment. I hadn't had many experiences in which honesty had led to grace and forgiveness. Honesty in such instances only ever led to harsh punishment and abuse.

Deception and the Cycle of Sabotage

As a third step in the cycle sabotaging our relationships, deception plays two key roles. The first role is to keep up appearances. When we feel we can't live up to the expectations of others, we use deception to fool them and gain their approval. We hide struggles, exaggerate successes, and pretend to be the person we think they want us to be.

The second role deception plays is for protection. That's the role it played for me in this story. Deception is a false form of relational protection. It tells us, "You can get away with it this time. They don't have to know. Next time you can get it right and everything will be fine." It's a false form of relational protection because to feel safe, we must put more distance between ourselves and others *without them knowing.*

In her book *The Complete ACOA Sourcebook*, Janet Woititz explains that one of the common characteristics of adult children of parents with alcoholism is lying when it doesn't provide any benefit.[1] As children, we grew accustomed to lying in a variety of forms. The lie at the center of the dysfunction was our family's denial of the problem. This implicitly taught us that lying for the sake of appearances was okay.[2] We saw this lie in the form of one parent covering for another's behavior or making excuses for why they couldn't show up.

We also experienced this dishonesty in our family of origin when promises were made that were never fulfilled. In this way, these promises turned out to be lies. What could never be spoken, however, was the truth of our situation.

Now, as adults, we may find ourselves in situations where we're tempted to lie when it'd be just as easy to tell the truth. However, our history has taught us that if it's okay to be deceptive, we might as well lie to ensure the best outcome. This inclination to cover ourselves or others for the sake of appearances is exacerbated by a culture that rewards the appearance of perfection. The mentality is, dishonesty is acceptable if it's going to enable us to achieve our goals. Lying is acceptable if it advances our careers. Deception is acceptable if it gets that person to date us.

This dishonesty was once a survival mechanism to escape excessive punishment. It's now become our mode of operation to manage appearances in our friendships, marriages, and work relationships. Though at one time lying made our lives safer, it became a habit we do naturally, even in circumstances where it no longer offers us any real benefit—hence, when it would be just as easy to tell the truth.

This is so painful because we struggle to differentiate our simple human flaws from the shame and guilt of hiding our parents' dysfunction. As a result, we feel a need to cover it all.

First, in relationships, this means we guess what others want us to say rather than saying what we really feel. Our conviction is compromised by our need to meet the expectations of others. The fear of disappointing someone significant in our life is unbearable. Lying is better than being unloved.

Secondly, we find ourselves taking on tasks, projects, and assignments we don't know how to do because we assume we should already know how to do them. To admit that we don't know is to appear incompetent. Incompetence is worse than dishonesty to the adult child of dysfunctional circumstances.

What Once Kept Us Alive Now Keeps Us from Feeling Alive

One of the great casualties of our difficult childhood was the joy of being ourselves. When we were children, deception was a fort we had to build to protect ourselves. But now it's become a prison. We are trapped in dishonesty as an outgrown coping skill, but we also don't know how to stop. We may carry the shame of how wrong it feels and how it destroys our relationships, but we don't know another way.

This experience connects us to the fallout of the original deception. The serpent deceived Eve, she took the fruit, and she and Adam ate. Out of fear, they hid from God, shifted blame, and shaded the truth. But shame was behind all of that. They were overwhelmed with shame about who they were when they were naked. They had lost the joy of being themselves.

Hiding was their protection, but then it became their prison. They were trapped in deception but didn't know another way. It was a tortured existence.

We know this existence well. Once hiding kept us safe and alive. But now it keeps us from feeling alive. Now it keeps us from experiencing life. It keeps us from the joy of being ourselves. I want to invite you out of the dark of that prison and into the light and freedom of being known as you are. Yes, it's true that in the safety of darkness, others can't see who you really are. But it's also true that in darkness, you can't see yourself well either.

How Dishonesty Hurts *Us*

Dishonesty ultimately hurts us because relationships play an essential role in our mental and emotional well-being. Your life has concentric circles of relationships at varying degrees of intimacy. The closer a relationship is to you, the greater determination it has on your well-being. If a relationship at work is suffering, but my relationship with my spouse or partner is good, I'm okay. It may be hard, but I'm okay.

However, if all my relationships at work are great, but my relationship with my partner is struggling, no number of good relationships at work is going to compensate for the pain I feel in the relationship with my partner. That's because this relationship is one of the closest to me and therefore has an exponential impact on my mental and emotional well-being.

The reason we don't have to be caught in our duplicity to be harmed by it is that our duplicity causes us to put distance between us and our intimate relationship. The catch is, we have to put distance in the relationship without telling them why we've put it there. And we do so hoping they won't discover it. That distance conceals the dishonesty. But it also compromises the integrity of the relationship. The gaps in honesty are like air pockets in a concrete foundation. Eventually the weight of what's built on top of them will expose them, and the cracks will begin to show up in other places.

A friend of mine shared the story of his struggling relationship with his brother. The relationship struggled because my friend had developed a lot of frustration over things that had happened in their childhood. As we discussed the relationship a few years later, he was able to see that a major driving force behind the distance in their relationship wasn't events from the past but the fear of his brother finding out who he really was. My friend had begun to struggle with a substance use disorder but wanted to preserve his appearance in his brother's eyes. As a result, he had to put distance between them to prevent him from finding out. He obviously couldn't say that's why he'd put distance between them, so he had to find another reason to justify the distance—anger because of things that happened in their childhood.

This deception was devastating to my friend because it had corroded a significant relationship in his life, causing increased isolation and loneliness. His anger consumed him, but it also had to be maintained to keep the relationship at arm's length. The anger and isolation drove greater substance use, and the distance allowed him to hide his substance use disorder, exacerbating its negative impact. Finally, it kept my friend trapped in the anxiety of keeping up an image. The devastation this caused him was real without his ever being "caught." In fact, it was precisely because he wasn't caught that his dishonesty was destroying his life.

So, What Do We Do?

Even if we can see how we use deception to keep up appearances or as relational protection, that knowledge alone does very little to change this entrenched behavior. We must take on some tools to reverse course on this way of relating to others.

Our Inclination to Hide Is Our Indication Not to Lie

The first thing I personally have done to address this is that I now take the inclination I feel to hide as an indication to do the opposite. It's the sign that I'm trying to be someone other than myself.

One experience that always creates immense anxiety for me is not knowing the answer but feeling like I should. It causes me to think, *If I'm any good at what I do, I should know the answer to this.* This happens in the workplace, as a parent, as a team leader, and on and on. In response to this anxiety, I fumble my words in search of an answer that sounds coherent, all the while thinking to myself, *I have no idea what I'm talking about.*

The honest answer in this moment is "That's a good question. I don't know," and this has now become a cue for me. When my initial thought is *I don't know. I need to come up with something,* that's my cue to say instead, "I don't know." Let the impulse to be dishonest become the indication that it's time to tell the truth.

What Do I Hope to Gain from This Dishonesty?

Secondly, before responding in those moments when I feel an inclination to be dishonest, I practice asking, "What do I really want?" Some of us have become accustomed to adapting our answers to everyone around us because we believe this dishonesty will provide something for us.

In moments when I feel a need to make up an answer, what I really want is to give an impression of competence. Ironically, fumbling my words in search of an answer often has the *opposite* effect—I sound incompetent. In my mind that's better than saying "I don't know." What's worse, this pretension costs me what I thought it had gained me—actual competence. Pretending I know prevents me from asking what I don't know. Being honest with myself about what I hope to gain from my dishonesty helps me see more clearly whether this deception is really getting me what I want in the first place.

Why Does Honesty Feel Like a Risk?

Third, I've begun asking, "Why does being honest here feel like a risk? What's at stake in my being honest?" Often what's at risk is some aspect of my identity that I want to portray for myself.

One aspect of my identity that I often base my value on is being a good leader. At times, I've based too much of my value on this being true. As a result, it feels like a tremendous risk to be honest when I don't know what to do. Because what kind of leader doesn't have all the answers? If I say, "I don't know," I will be exposed as the bad leader I really am, and the house of cards holding up my appearance of value will crumble.

The truth is, no one can be expected to have all the answers. And so what's respected more than having all the answers is being transparent when we don't. This empowers my team, for example, to contribute to the solution and to feel like a valuable part of the project. I've also discovered that my team has greater buy-in on the execution of a solution when they have been a part of the problem-solving.

Maybe for you it's maintaining the image of a good parent, a great teacher, a perfect spouse, or an outstanding coworker. Chances are that maintaining this aspect of your identity has made it difficult to own your mistakes, acknowledge when you need help, or accept that you don't know all the answers.

Persistent Dishonesty Only Makes Things Worse

Fourth, an important piece of reversing this habit is understanding that persisting in hiding is most detrimental to myself. I most negatively impact myself through this dishonesty because I become a prisoner to the false image I've constructed around myself. A false image that, from now on, I must keep up.

This follows naturally from the last exercise, but it's helpful to name the harm that this dishonesty does us. When the distance between who we are and the identity we want to portray becomes too great, dishonesty and duplicity become essential to keeping it up. In these instances, honesty risks letting that image fall. The truth is, it would be so freeing if it did.

Maintaining this image is not only exhausting, but it also prevents us from growing and improving. It keeps us from being the best parent, spouse, employee, etc., because it's difficult to grow in areas where we're not honest about our need to grow. Consequently, we remain hidden behind a false image of ourselves. The exhaustion of holding up this false image always catches up with us—and often in ways that exacerbate the embarrassment we'd hoped to avoid all along.

What If We're Wrong?

Finally, it's been extremely helpful to ask, "What if my guess about what they want from me is wrong?" What if what others want from you is exactly who you are, not somebody else?

The truth is, if it's not you they want, you can't ultimately give them what they want anyway. Wouldn't it be freeing to stop pretending? To not have to pretend in the first place? We spend so much energy and emotional stress on trying to be someone we *think* others want us to be without ever asking ourselves, "What if what they really want is just for me to be who I am?"

We've lived for so long with the belief that who we are isn't enough. Who we are isn't what those around us want. This makes it difficult to accept that our perceived weaknesses are part of who we need to be in order to do what God wants with our lives. The longer it takes for us to accept this, the longer we postpone the joy of being content in ourselves. Who knows what's riding on you being who God created you to be!

At the end of the day, the fort we built with dishonesty to protect ourselves has become a prison that now traps us. Once it was necessary. Once it kept us safe and alive. But now it keeps us from feeling alive.

True relational protection can only be found in appropriate boundaries. Our challenge is to respect ourselves enough to set them and require others to accept them.

7

BOUNDARIES

Isn't It Selfish to Respect Myself?

Beth reached out to me for some guidance on a situation unfolding in her life. As we sat in my office, I listened as she shared the harrowing story of her violent twenty-year marriage. Her husband had battled severe substance abuse and as a result had infused their marriage with tumult and chaos.

She went to a women's shelter for protection, and he served a sentence in prison for domestic abuse. After their divorce, Beth's ex-husband moved in with her sister Stephanie, who eventually married him as well. Beth tried to warn Stephanie about what kind of husband he had been and what kind of marriage they'd had, but Stephanie was unwilling to listen. Beth's warnings were interpreted as jealousy, severing her relationship with her sister and eventually rifting the entire family. Stephanie later divorced this man as well.

The relationship between Beth and Stephanie remained broken until recently. Beth's beloved uncle passed away and left some things to her. Believing that Stephanie might be interested in some of the items, Beth sent some of them to her sister. Quite unexpectedly, Stephanie interpreted this act as reopening the door to their relationship and a sign that all was forgiven. Her sister began texting her frequently and even invited herself over to spend some time together.

Beth was struggling to understand the call to forgive as a Christian. Because she was a sincere follower of Jesus, she questioned what her responsibility was in pursuing healing and reconciliation in their relationship. She was anxious about suffering further hurt and the potential abuses of trusting her sister again.

As I began telling her what I thought she ought to do, it dawned on me that everything I was advising her to do depended on one thing—her ability to respect herself. I knew this was going to be difficult, because spending nearly twenty years married to a person with alcoholism corrodes your self-respect and, consequently, your ability to maintain boundaries and resist manipulation. This, too, is a consequence of the codependency we discussed in chapter 4.

Boundary Issues and the Cycle of Sabotage

The fourth and final element in the cycle of sabotage is boundary issues. Relational boundaries that are clearly communicated and regularly enforced are the appropriate form of relational protection.

Boundaries can protect us from manipulation; invasions of privacy; emotional, verbal, and physical abuse; unrealistic expectations; overbearing family members; disrespectful employers; and all matter of relational dysfunction. However, just as we are coming to the moment in the cycle where our solution ought to be enforcing boundaries, our codependency won't let us. This is the whole reason it's called the *cycle* of sabotage.

Early in ministry, I thought I was supposed to be available to people whenever they needed something. That's what makes people say, "He's such a great pastor!" Unfortunately, what made me such a great pastor was making me a not-so-present husband and father. I was caught in the cycle of sabotage. I didn't really know who I was, so I defined myself according to what made me valuable to others (codependency and approval seeking). When I began to burn out from exhaustion, I gave excuses for why I couldn't be available to people, and I tried to cover up my absence with my family by texting and emailing when no one was looking. I'd escape to the bathroom and take a little too long to respond to an email. "My stomach's just upset," I'd say. Worse, I would schedule two meetings in one evening but explain that the first ran long because I knew two meetings in one evening was unacceptable (deception).

I needed to communicate and enforce some boundaries, but fear got the best of me. *What if people get upset? What if people are mad at me because I'm not available to them? What if they say I'm a bad pastor? What if they tell all their friends I'm a bad pastor?*

At the very moment I needed boundaries, I was too afraid to enforce them. This was because I didn't know who I was apart from the role I played in their lives and the approval it gained me. I shrouded my boundary issues in self-sacrificial logic. The real issue was that I lacked the self-respect to enforce boundaries.

What Is Self-Respect?

When we talk about respect between two people, we are referring to the awareness that each of us is an autonomous entity with our own physical, mental, and emotional "property." When we respect each other, we acknowledge that we cannot transgress the boundaries of the other person's property and simply do with their property as we see fit.

By self-respect, then, we mean extending that same recognition to ourselves. We have our own physical, mental, and emotional property with boundaries that ought not be transgressed. These are boundaries we shouldn't be asked or forced to relinquish.

One of the most painful consequences of my own parents' marriage has been watching my mother struggle to regain the sense of self-respect that was taken from her by her struggle to love and support my father out of his addiction. There's no easy answer as to how to love someone with an addiction, especially when they have their own painful story of why and how they came to addiction.

In my father's case, he'd grown up with an overbearing father who was brutally harsh, critical, and demanding. There was no room for mistakes, and a failure to obey always resulted in painful punishment. This produced an incredible work ethic in my father. What other choice did he have? He became driven to achieve, work long hours, and obey the demands of the critical voice in his head that mimicked the voice of his father: "You're worthless if you can't do this right. Keep working and maybe you'll be worth something."

As my father lay in a bed at UNC Hospital near the end of his life, we had one of the few honest conversations we ever had about his drinking. He shared that he hadn't really started drinking until after college, but when he began working in agriculture, he and his coworkers would sometimes work thirty-six hours or more without sleep, and drinking was how they kept going.

I suspect the alcohol was as much for numbing the shaming voice in his head that told him he was still worthless as it was for fighting the sleep he so desperately needed.

I share all this to say that in a relationship with a person you love, it's difficult to know when you're being confided in with tremendous vulnerability and when you're being manipulated by a painful story. In sympathy, I believe my mom wanted to help him. But to do so, she had to allow her own mental and emotional boundaries to be crossed.

How Do We Lose Self-Respect?

Over time, the slight but repeated nicks to our clarity about addictive behavior and our role in the addict's life corrode our understanding of what it means to love them well. These things diminish our ability to love ourselves well. What feels like the loving and compassionate thing to do can in fact require us to set aside what's healthy for ourselves, as well as what's a good and healthy boundary in the relationship.

Before we know it, we find ourselves making all kinds of decisions and excuses for all kinds of our own behavior. Those standing outside the situation can see clearly that the manipulation is unacceptable, unhealthy, and completely in-defensible. But inside the situation, the manipulation distorts our thinking so much that we lose all orientation for what's self-respecting and what's not.

Chances are this manipulation began before we even had a chance to develop self-respect. We were already being ma-nipulated into behavior that distorted our clarity about what we were deserving of or what was inappropriate and unac-ceptable. To this day I still struggle to have a clear category for self-respect because it feels so at odds with loving people around me.

This is precisely the problem. We grew up in environ-ments that taught us that self-respecting behavior was at odds with loving the people around us. Somehow *self-respect* became conflated with *selfishness*, and selfishness was un-acceptable. This is truly ironic given that the dysfunctional adult or adults in our lives were completely absorbed in their own worlds, problems, and needs, and they demanded— sometimes violently—that we acquiesce to their notion of reality. We now carry this misinformed conflation into our relationships and find it extremely difficult to discern how to simultaneously love those around us and have respect for ourselves in the process.

For Beth, whose story I shared at the beginning of this chapter, it would've been easy to cave to the belief that she doesn't really need to have an honest conversation with her sister about what she needs because Stephanie might not respond well and the relationship won't be restored. In the end, it'll be Beth's fault because she asked something of her sister that she shouldn't have. According to her family of origin, the loving thing to do would be to drop it and just pretend like it didn't happen for the sake of having a relationship.

This, however, isn't how a healthy, mutual relationship works. This is asking Beth to set aside pain that needs to be addressed—but not for the sake of the relationship. The relationship will be hurt and more dysfunctional if this is set aside. No, Beth is being asked to set this aside in the interest of Stephanie's selfish desire to avoid discomfort or acknowledging wrongdoing.

We accept different kinds of manipulated narratives when self-respect and love are taught to be at odds with each other.

You Will Always Love Your Neighbor the Way You Love Yourself

When Jesus was challenged to recall the greatest commandment, he responded, "Love the Lord your God with all your heart and with all your soul and with all your mind" (Matt. 22:37 NIV). The religious authorities of Jesus's day sought every opportunity to test him and catch him in error to discredit his claim as the Messiah. Jesus saw through their veiled attempt to dismantle his credibility and seized this opportunity to remind them of another crucial commandment: love your neighbor as yourself (Lev. 19:18; Matt. 22:39).

Jesus wanted to remind them that perfect obedience to the greatest commandment includes obedience to this second greatest command—to love your neighbor as yourself—which, by the way, they weren't doing by attempting to discredit and trap Jesus in error.

This command to love your neighbor as yourself contains a crucial element we often overlook when thinking about what it means to love the manipulative people in our lives: we're commanded to love our neighbor *as ourselves*.

Jesus isn't asking us to act unloving toward ourselves in the work of loving others. In fact, to love our neighbor well, we must understand how to love ourselves well. Loving ourselves informs how we love others.

This isn't a "me first" manipulation of Jesus's teaching. This is a corrective to our distorted idea that loving others means disrespecting ourselves. The truth is quite the opposite: we can't love our neighbor well if we don't love and respect ourselves well in the first place.

When I love others without respect for myself, my love for them ultimately becomes fear-based, self-serving, and manipulative: How can I love them in a way that gains their approval or avoids their rejection? This isn't love. It's codependency.

In the end, we will always love our neighbor in the same way that we love ourselves.

What's Good for You Is Also Good for Them

As adult children from dysfunctional families, we aren't known for treating ourselves very well. It's true, whether it's through the things we put into our bodies to numb our pain or the thoughts we have about ourselves because of this pain.

If we don't know how to act lovingly toward ourselves, how can we hope to love others well? This isn't to disparage us. This is to challenge the notion that we instinctively know how to love others well. How we think we love people often requires us to set aside our needs and well-being. When we cave to the manipulation and enable another's mistreatment of us to continue, we also set aside their needs and well-being. Their deepest need in that moment is to learn how to function in healthy, nonmanipulative ways.

Just because challenging their manipulation wouldn't feel good to them doesn't mean it's not loving to them. Likewise, just because it'd be hard for us to stand up to them doesn't mean it's not loving toward ourselves. In such instances, the most loving thing for them is also the most loving and self-respecting thing for us.

This is incredibly counterintuitive for us, but it's precisely the kind of thinking we've lost the ability to do because we lived for so long under the reality-manipulating indoctrination of our dysfunctional childhood.

So, What Do We Do?

The work required to regain self-respect and enforce boundaries involves two key shifts in our approach to relationships. One is a shift in thinking, another is a shift in what we require of relationships.

Unlink Some Ideas in Your Thinking

The first idea we must unlink is: what feels loving to others = loving others. As adult children of difficult circumstances, we may be extremely sensitive to what we believe our actions will make others feel—and for good reason. As children, the way we made a parent feel may have determined how harshly they treated us. However, now as adults we trip all over ourselves to make sure no one feels bad because of anything we say or do.

One consequence of this is that we equate what's loving to others with what makes others *feel loved*. This is all well and good when we're talking about acts of kindness to strangers or when it comes to understanding the "love languages" of significant people in our lives. However, when it comes to the unhealthy relationships or unhealthy people in our lives, what makes them "feel loved" may not be the best thing for them or the relationship at all.

In my own parents' relationship, my dad's feelings of not being loved by his parents became a heavy weight around my mother's neck. She feared that if she made him feel unloved, he'd accuse her of being just like his parents. This was true even though they were very different circumstances. This made it difficult for my mom to know what to do because of the tension that existed between what felt loving to my father and what was the most loving thing to do for him.

What was actually loving was allowing him to suffer the consequences of his alcoholism so that he might ultimately get help to get better. However, holding someone accountable, or not "rescuing" someone, doesn't always feel very loving to the one being held accountable. We must decouple the equation that what feels loving to others *is* loving to others.

A second equation we must unlink is the assumption that sacrifice entails disrespecting ourselves. This is the idea that if I'm going to sacrifice for someone, I'm going to have to disrespect myself—that is what sacrifice is. But I think we need to dig down a couple of layers on this.

Our childhood environment didn't do much to help us distinguish between selfishness and self-respect. In fact, it may have forged a hard equation between the two. Things we were forced to endure as a child drove us to believe that demanding others to respect us was selfish. Because this belief was forged before we even had a chance to develop a clear sense of self-respect, it's nearly impossible to develop now. We're not recovering something we once had; we're trying to develop a tool we've lacked and compensated for our entire lives.

When we do examine what's entailed in this assumption, we see with new clarity the major difference between sacrificing our time, money, energy, attention, availability, and even dreams or lifelong plans and being asked to do something we believe is wrong, self-degrading, or dismissive of our well-being. It isn't sacrificial to endure emotional, physical, or sexual abuse. It's also not selfish to demand that people respect our humanity. It's one thing to choose to give of ourselves freely; it's something altogether different to believe that if we don't give these things, we'll be punished.

Require Your Relationships to Be Reciprocal

There's no doubt that relationships, like marriage, require sacrifice. But whether it's marriage or a relationship with a sibling, friend, or coworker, in a healthy relationship the sacrifices are reciprocated.

This means one of you in the relationship isn't the only one who always apologizes to make the relationship work. Instead, both of you apologize when apologies are needed. It means one of you isn't the only one who takes responsibility for problems in the relationship to smooth things over and keep the peace. Instead, you or the other person take responsibility at the appropriate times when you or they are genuinely responsible for problems in the relationship.

I advised Beth to explain to her sister that she'd like to reopen the possibility of a relationship, but to do that, there were a few things she needed Stephanie to understand. Beth needed her to understand how painful it was that she hadn't believed her and chose her ex-husband's side, even to the point of marrying him. She needed Stephanie to help repair relationships with family members she had turned against Beth. She needed Stephanie to own her slanderous comments that pitted the family against Beth.

Beth doubted her sister would receive these needs very well and would most likely get defensive. I explained to Beth that if that was the case, Stephanie really didn't want a relationship with her again—at least not a healthy one. If the relationship depended on Beth setting aside her needs or being silent about past hurt, they were trying to rebuild their relationship on a broken foundation. It was broken because Beth was carrying more of the emotional weight than Stephanie was.

It was also important for Beth to understand that she must not be manipulated into believing that she was the one preventing the relationship just because she asked for this hurt to be acknowledged and these boundaries to be respected.

There's a way of narrating this request as Beth preventing the relationship from happening because she isn't "letting the past be the past." However, this narration requires Beth to disrespect her own pain and boundaries by asking her to do all the emotional work for the relationship to exist. This isn't reciprocal. This is a one-sided relationship. Therefore, it's important to make it clear that if Stephanie isn't willing to acknowledge Beth's hurt feelings and respect her boundaries, then she's the one preventing the relationship. This is true regardless of how Stephanie would like to narrate reality.

Boundaries and Reciprocal Relationships

In their bestselling book *Boundaries*, Henry Cloud and John Townsend share that there are four kinds of people who struggle with boundaries: (1) those who are unable to set boundaries, (2) those who are unable to respect boundaries, (3) those who set boundaries against responsibility to love others, and (4) those who set boundaries against receiving love.[1]

When we think of struggles with boundaries, we typically think of the first one. However, it's also crucially important to recognize when someone is unable or unwilling to respect your boundaries.

On the one hand, this kind of boundary offense is narrated to make you feel guilty for having boundaries, as if you're the problem. This is manipulation. On the other hand, if you find yourself struggling to accept other people's boundaries, you may need to ask yourself if you're demanding more of others in the relationship than you're willing to give. Must people regularly set aside their boundaries to be in relationship with you? This isn't a reciprocal relationship. In a truly reciprocal relationship, you never have to wonder if the other person is looking out for you. You and the other person respect each other's boundaries. They don't make you feel guilty for having boundaries, and you don't pressure them to sacrifice theirs.

For some of us who internalized the pain of our childhood, we may feel that we must always give more than we receive to be loved. For those of us who externalized this pain, we believe others must demonstrate their love by constantly overextending themselves for us.[2]

In her book *Adult Children of Emotionally Immature Parents*, Lindsay Gibson lists several characteristics of emotionally mature people in reciprocal relationships. In addition to respecting our boundaries, they give back, they're flexible and compromise well, they're even-tempered, they're willing to be influenced, they're truthful, they apologize, and they make amends.[3] This may feel like quite an unfamiliar description of the people we've found ourselves in relationship with.

When we come into relationship with such emotionally mature people, we realize we've never known what it's like for someone to be disappointed without holding it against us. We don't have any experience telling someone no and hearing them say okay without an ounce of guilt in it. We brace for impact when we've seriously messed something up, only to find ourselves shocked when someone responds gently.

Experiencing Respect Can Be Confusing

As eight-year-old boys full of imagination, my friend and I found ourselves wrapped up in pretending to build an epic bonfire in the woods near my childhood home. We were pouring all kinds of flammable concoctions onto the fire, breaking apart sticks, setting them up just so, and pretending to set them ablaze. In reality, the flammable concoctions were mostly just toothpaste and ketchup.

The wood we were breaking up turned out to be a very valuable antique wagon that belonged to my father. I don't even remember if my friend was sent home before the cussing, insults, and awful whipping began. I still find myself getting overwhelmed with the emotion of that moment as I recall that this "precious antique" was just sitting in the woods rotting under pine straw and leaves.

Fast-forward fifteen years, and my in-laws-to-be had just moved into a brand-new condo. During one of my first visits, I rolled an ottoman across their beautiful hardwood floor. What I thought were perfectly good rollers turned out to be stubbornly jammed wheels that left behind a scratch the length of my arm. My immediate instinct was to roll the otto-man back over the scratch and pretend like nothing happened.

If my childhood had taught me anything, the punishment for this damage would be brutal. At the same time, I knew that if the scratch was discovered, the fact that I had lied about it would only make it worse. I didn't know what to do. It was an awful position to be in as someone who wanted to please his future in-laws but also didn't want to found our relationship on lies!

I finally owned up to defacing their property and braced for the backlash. But it didn't come. I had anticipated anger, ridicule, insults, and disappointment. I was met instead with a simple "It's okay. It won't be the last time it gets scratched."

I was completely stunned and, quite honestly, confused. Where was the anger? Where were the insults? I didn't know what to do without the familiar pain of overreaction. Was this how "normal" people handled these things? Was this what a proportional response looked like?

On the one hand, it was beautiful and freeing. On the other hand, it was almost awkward and uncomfortable. Didn't I need to be punished? Could we really be okay if they didn't yell at me a little? I'd never experienced an even-tempered, appropriate response from a father-type figure in my life, and it took a long time for me to process just how radically different this was from the reality I knew as a child.

Growing into a reciprocal relationship full of mutual respect is extremely hard when we've never known that kind of relationship. It's not just hard for us; we also have a way of making it hard for others. They don't transgress our boundaries, and we confuse that with being distant. They allow space for us to make decisions for ourselves, and we flounder in our indecision. They ask our opinion, and we fumble because we've never been allowed to have one. They apologize and we freeze because we don't know what to do when someone acknowledges that they've wronged us. We don't know how to receive because all we've ever done is give.

Contrary to what our childhood experiences taught us, it isn't selfish to respect ourselves. What our childhood taught us wasn't selflessness; it was self-disrespect. Selflessness is a virtue we offer of our own free will. Self-disrespect is a reaction driven by fear.

Boundaries Are Key

A lack of boundaries perpetuates the cycle that sabotages our relationships. Learning to establish boundaries is the key to stopping it. I invite you to discuss boundaries with your counselor and check out resources like *Boundaries* by Henry Cloud and John Townsend. Setting boundaries will help you overcome codependency, which will free you from the pursuit of others' approval; and not needing others' approval will remove the necessity to appear to be anyone other than yourself.

PT 3 | THE GOOD BAGGAGE WORKING TOGETHER FOR OUR RELATIONSHIPS NOW

Now that we've identified the cycle of sabotage and how it's undermining our relationships, we can move to the good news: the good things our childhood put in us. We'll take an in-depth look at six aspects of the good baggage we carry and how they can work together for the benefit of our relationships now.

In chapter 3, we highlighted the passion for healthy relationships that our childhood put in us. When we leverage this passion, we begin to see the impact of our childhood in a different light. There is much to overcome, but there is also much to uncover.

We'll begin by looking at how the things that make us different uniquely prepare us for healthy relationships. We'll then discover specific strengths packed in our baggage. These strengths include our relational intentionality, our empathy, our loyalty, our responsible nature, and our romantic instincts. Each of these gifts is good on its own. But when we learn how they can work together, we discover the exceptional relationships our childhood prepared us for.

8

A UNIQUE PERSPECTIVE

What Makes Us Different Doesn't Make Us Bad

The greatest trigger of insecurity for me as a pastor is when what feels instinctive for me is so different from what other pastors are doing. This is especially true when I look at famous pastors who are known to have the most success. Initially my response was to simply mimic what I saw others do. After all, it seemed to work for them, right? But over time I began to feel a dissonance between what felt true to myself and what I felt compelled to do because it was what others were doing. I realized that if I continued to mimic what others did, I'd burn out trying to be something I wasn't. I was exhausted trying to be someone else but too afraid of failing to be myself.

If this sounds familiar to you, it won't be surprising that this also has been identified as a common characteristic of children who grew up in dysfunctional families. It's common for those of us with difficult childhoods to feel that we're different from everyone else.

Why We Feel Different

As children, we felt different because we were unable to be truly carefree and playful. We could never be fully present where we were because we were concerned about what might be happening at home. We were preparing for what kind of situation we might walk into when we got there.

On top of this, because we didn't know what normal was, we often felt awkward. This drove us either to isolate because we felt so different or to master social cues and behaviors to mask our feelings. To this day, I find myself extraordinarily sensitive to the awkwardness of any moment. I'll say the same thing over and over in the same conversation or ask the same question twice just to avoid the awkwardness of silence.

We also lived with a fear that what made us different would lead to rejection or abandonment. This made us do some unusual things. We'd give away some of our most prized possessions and beloved toys just to have others engage with us. Others of us found it easier to isolate altogether. I personally developed a "counter-dependence." In reaction to the fear of being overly dependent, I insisted on self-reliance even when support was available to me.

We also felt different because, to some degree, we just were. We were different because our parents couldn't get it together enough to engage us in extracurricular activities. We were different because a parent's debilitating illness required so much care, we didn't receive the attention necessary to develop our confidence. We were different because our parent with a disability made it difficult for us to have "normal" childhood experiences, such as summer vacations, concerts, cross-country trips, or simply a bedtime story.

We were different because maybe as kids we had to act like a parent and take care of our brothers and sisters. Maybe we lived in fear of abuse. Maybe we lived with such horrific scenarios at home that we couldn't even bring ourselves to tell our closest friends at school. We had stepbrothers or stepsisters who insisted on touching us inappropriately or men in our house who treated us as objects for their pleasure. We were different because we lived in a home full of anger, but no one ever knew it.

We may not have experienced all this, but what we did experience did make us different.

This feeling of being different produced immense insecurity, uncertainty, self-loathing depression, anxiety, and a loss of identity, and some of us harmed ourselves. In some cases, it even drove us to the edge of taking our own lives. This only exacerbated the distance we felt, to the point that we doubted whether we could be accepted as we are at all.

The Impact on Our Identity

Those of us who grew up in a dysfunctional family share the struggle to have a clear sense of our identity. As I've said, this is due in part to the fact that we kept the peace by being who those around us wanted us to be. As a result, it was difficult to know when we were being ourselves versus who others wanted us to be. This pressure to be someone other than ourselves was in addition to already feeling different and was exacerbated by not having a clear sense of who we were in the first place.

A great challenge for me as a pastor has been accepting that God called *me* to be a pastor, not who I think I should be. I've wrestled with who I think I should preach like, who I should lead like, who I should write like, counsel like, tweet like, Instagram like, and on and on and on. It's incredibly difficult to lean into who you are when it feels like you're so different from the successful people around you. You constantly doubt yourself, asking, *Is it okay to be me?*

The truth is, a lot is at stake in you being you. In fact, the good baggage you bring to your relationships depends on it.

How Do We Leverage Being Different?

We leverage this feeling of being different when we lean into it for the good things it can provide us. First, being different offers a shift in perspective. *Different* sounds negative, but Scripture is clear that our unique design is a gift. Rather than attempt to conceal the differences, lean into what makes you unique.

Paul begins chapter 12 of his first letter to the Corinthians by calling out a crucial change that takes place when we live in the power of God's Spirit: we begin to see ourselves as a part of something bigger than ourselves. Paul writes, "You know that when you were pagans, you used to be enticed and led astray by mute idols" (v. 2). Paul was speaking about literal wooden figures that represented false gods. They couldn't even speak, yet what they promised made it irresistible to worship them. For example, if you worshiped the idol for the god of fertility, it'd help ensure that you had lots of children.

This imagery creates a sharp critique of modern-day idolatry. Idolatry for us today isn't so much worshiping depictions of false gods. Idolatry is giving our whole life in pursuit of something because of what we believe it'll give us. We pursue success, fame, wealth, or popularity because we believe it'll provide us a sense of significance, security, superiority, peace, prosperity, comfort, and on and on. These modern idols tell us that if we just work hard enough, they'll give us everything we ever wanted.

I'm concerned that these modern idols are the greatest obstacles to people discovering their unique place in the body of Christ and fulfilling the role they were created to play in God's kingdom. The world has a way of telling us which parts of the body are most important. These typically correlate with what functions in our imagination as being necessary to achieve things like success. But in the pursuit of success, we attempt to manifest the gift we believe will get us there rather than the one we were given to uniquely contribute to the body.

The gift we believe will get us there is usually the same one that got someone else there. This encourages conformity and uniformity. It's only when we put off these false idols that we become free to find the life-giving place we were created for. It's often once we embrace what makes us different that we also embrace the unique role it equips us to play in the body of Christ. Once again, gifting and our sense of living go together. We can also add our sense of meaning to that. When we're operating in our gifting, we experience a fuller sense of living and fulfill our God-given meaning.

Paul goes on to explain *how* we are a part of something bigger than ourselves:

> For just as the body is one and has many parts, and all the parts of that body, though many, are one body—so also is [the body of] Christ. . . . If the foot should say, "Because I'm not a hand, I don't belong to the body," it is not for that reason any less a part of the body. . . . The eye cannot say to the hand, "I don't need you!" Or again, the head can't say to the feet, "I don't need you!" (vv. 12, 15, 21)

Some of us, like the foot, might say, "I'm not a hand, so what am I worth?" forgetting all along that the body cannot walk without its feet. Others of us, like the mouth, may say, "What can the body do without me? I'm everything!" forgetting that the mouth depends on the lungs for the very breath it uses to speak. The point here is not that we're all the most important but that the most important thing we can be is the part of the body we were created to be. The interdependency of this body tells us this crucial truth: *every part of the body matters, but no part is enough on its own.*

Paul insists, "But as it is, God has arranged each one of the parts in the body just as he wanted" (v. 18). Just as *he* wanted. We come to understand the freedom of this when we trust that God's plan for our lives is better than our plan for our lives. When gifting, living, and meaning line up, it's better than anything our current pursuits can give us.

I love that Paul makes it a point to say that those parts of the body that are weaker are in fact indispensable (v. 22). You are indispensable. You are different and you are unique—and that makes you indispensable.

The corollary to this is that what makes you unique may reveal your calling. As I wrestled with the ways I felt different from the pastors around me and eventually grew exhausted with trying to be someone I wasn't, I finally leaned into what I was good at and what was life-giving to me: relationships and counseling.

I've always enjoyed the one-on-one part of ministry far more than the big crowd or the "Sunday show." I finally accepted what I enjoyed instead of pretending to enjoy the parts I didn't but thought I was supposed to. I love helping people have aha moments about their lives, their relationships, and God. None of this was glamorous or especially Instagrammable, but it was meaningful for the people whom God had entrusted to me.

I also acknowledged the painful things that happened in my childhood. I sought a deeper understanding of how they were continuing to shape me as an adult, a husband, a father, a pastor, and a friend. As you can now well see, I found that it wasn't only for bad that these things happened, but that God, in his redeeming nature, could bring good from them—both for my sake and the sake of others.

Another way of saying this is that I discovered a new dimension of my calling. I realized an aspect of what God created me to do that I couldn't have learned if I hadn't accepted what made me different, weaker, less significant, insufficient, or whatever word you want to use to describe this feeling of the outsider we live with.

What many of us think is our limp is actually our life purpose. No one knows what it's like to limp except for the person who struggles with a limp. No one knows what it's like to overcome a stutter except for the one who has overcome a stutter. No one knows what it's like to leverage the pain of their childhood for the good of their adult relationships except for someone who has done it.

What's your limp? What does God want to do with it through your life?

Finally, this good baggage of feeling different prepares us for exceptional relationships because we can lean into where we feel like we're different as an investigative framework for discovering new areas for relational growth. One of the gifts of feeling different is that we aren't blinded to growth because we already fit the mold of "normal."

In moments when our feeling of being different is most intense, we can use that as an internal sensor to do some personal work.

Why am I feeling different?

Do I feel exposed in some way?

What is this feeling telling me about myself?

Is what feels different inherently bad or is it just not the accepted norm?

If so, what does this tell me about how to be healthy in this scenario?

How do I adjust my target from feeling normal to being healthy?

Does this feeling reveal something unique about who I am instead?

As I uncovered the many ways my childhood formed me and created problems in my relationships, my leadership, and my mental and emotional health, I became quite angry with my dad. I was mad because of how his alcoholism would continue to affect every aspect of my life long after he was gone.

After months and months of naming and changing patterns, habits, and obstacles, it finally dawned on me: this experience that makes me feel so different is also the thing that's put good things inside me. What if we could learn to leverage those good things for the sake of our relationships?

Prior to this moment, I carried a lot of anger for having to do all this extra work just to be normal. Because on top of all the normal challenges of life, I had this additional struggle of dealing with being an adult child of a dysfunctional family. Now my eyes had been opened, and my perspective had shifted to the gift of seeing things through a different lens. It's not that I was glad I'd been through what I had. But I discovered that what I had been through could be *redeemed*.

A Better Notion of Redemption

The concept of redemption is important for processing the trauma we experienced as children. Within Christian circles, a common approach to dealing with the pain of childhood is to find a way to explain how what happened to us happened for a reason. The mentality is that if we can find a reason why this happened, we can better accept it.

I have three problems with this. First, it means we're trying to justify completely unjustifiable actions and events. Some evil is beyond justification. Some of what we experienced can't be explained and shouldn't be explained beyond the fact that it's of the evil one. There's no good reason that these things happened, and we ought not to dignify them by giving them a reason.

Second, it makes God into the author of horrible, tragic, traumatic evil. Yes, there are hard things in our life that belong to the journey of faith that God is the author of. But God isn't the author of incest, abuse, addiction, neglect, or abandonment.

Third, the notion that God would have us go through something as painful as our childhood just to say, "But look, I have redeemed you" is a sham redemption. If I force you to undergo some painful experience, only to be waiting on the other side to rescue you, that is profoundly selfish and evil.

Instead, the concept of authentic redemption is so profound for our healing precisely because God didn't design the pain of our childhood but nevertheless is always working to redeem it. To redeem something is to take something we thought was lost, worthless, or beyond repair and infuse it with new purpose, value, and hope. God takes what we thought was the lost cause of our childhood and declares, "I want to do something with that pain. I want to heal it and use it for the healing of others."

God declares, "The experience that told you that you were worthless was a lie. You were molded and made under the eye of your Creator, and the good I placed in you hasn't been destroyed by the evil done to you."

God declares, "What you thought was beyond repair are the broken pieces I will use. The sacred wounds of your pain aren't scars but 'rebirth' marks, identifying the unique contribution you will make in my world."

With God, nothing is lost, worthless, or beyond repair. It's pain waiting on the promise of redemption.

9

RELATIONAL INTENTIONALITY

Channeling Our Emotional Intensity

In the immediate aftermath of Sharon discovering my substance use disorder, her concern for me increased her attention toward me. As she wept in fear for my mental and spiritual health, she was also much more verbally and physically affectionate than I could ever remember. This crisis had brought out a new emotional intensity in her, and I liked it. In normal times, when everything was going well, our marriage seemed to lack a certain emotional intensity that something in me craved. I was used to emotional intensity in my childhood, and when that was absent in my marriage, I thought something was wrong.

At first, I thought this was something that needed to change about our relationship. But as I processed this idea in light of what I was learning about children of dysfunctional families, I discovered that what I really craved was the familiarity of emotional intensity in a family environment. Though unhealthy, it produced the sense in me that this intensity was what characterized a passionate love relationship. What I failed to appreciate was the security, stability, and peace that the absence of this chaos afforded our marriage. I craved emotional intensity at the cost of the trust and stability of our relationship.

Although the chaos of our childhood created a certain craving for emotional intensity, this craving can also become a driver for relational intentionality. This is one of the ways that what makes us different isn't necessarily bad. As we work through this chapter, we'll come to understand how this relational intentionality can contribute to healthy relationships.

Comfortable with Chaos

Because our childhood produced chaos and turmoil, we developed a certain level of comfortability with a chaotic environment. So much so that many of us now begin to experience anxiety, depression, and fear in the *absence* of chaos. A chaotic environment triggers our survival mode. Survival mode heightens our brain's arousal and narrows its function in a way that quiets the rise of painful memories. This can be true to such a degree that "trauma survivors frequently create chaos in their lives to continue survival adaptation and avoid feeling pain."[1]

You'd think our response would be to avoid chaotic circumstances now that we have more control over our lives. But when we were children, the hostility, anger, abuse, or neglect kept us on high alert. This state of being on guard translated to a high level of physiological arousal—high heart rate, increased blood pressure, change in respiration rate, increased electrical activity in the brain—even as we attempted to deny the truth and pain of our circumstances. We attempted to deny with our mind what our body readily acknowledged. It was a coping mechanism with long-term, devastating effects.

One of those effects is our bodies' inability to cope with *not* being on high alert and arousal. Because we grew so accustomed to the pain, chaos, and unpredictable behavior of a dysfunctional environment, we now find ourselves experiencing immense anxiety in the absence of such environmental stimulation. Like elastic that's been stretched out, our bodies now demand a new level of arousal to continue to feel okay. This hyperarousal is what it feels like to be alive and real.

In his must-read work on trauma, *The Body Keeps the Score*, Bessel van der Kolk writes, "When you don't feel real nothing matters, which makes it impossible to protect yourself from danger. Or you may resort to extremes in an effort to feel something—even cutting yourself with a razor blade or getting into fistfights with strangers."[2] Because our normal was characterized by such immense pain, the absence of arousal and alertness now leaves us feeling nothing. As a result, our subconscious response is to do anything just to feel *something*.

Hurt So Good (Sometimes Love Don't Feel Like It Should)

It's almost cliché now, but we've all heard the line in shows "Why do I keep falling for people who treat me poorly?"

Maybe you'll find it helpful to know that there's a very good, even scientific, reason for this. A reason that can help us understand the subconscious impulses that drive us to these relationships over and over again.

In their book *A General Theory of Love*, Thomas Lewis, Fari Amini, and Richard Lannon offer one of the most compelling explanations of why we fall in love with the people we do.[3] A key aspect that determines who we fall in love with is the way the relationships of our childhood formed how our brain connects emotionally with others now. This is an extreme over-simplification, but the idea is that if you grew up in a context with very volatile relationships, the very makeup of your brain is going to develop a level of familiarity with that volatility. When we are an adult, our brain will prefer relationships that offer a similar experience as the relationships we experienced as children.

Lewis, Amini, and Lannon explain that at an early age, a child begins to "extract patterns from its relationships."[4] By this they mean that before we're even able to capture event memories, we "store impressions of what love *feels* like."[5] From this, our neural memory compresses these impressions and qualities into what they call *attractors*. From the accumulation of repeated imprints, a "concentrated knowledge whispers to a child from beneath the veil of consciousness, telling him what relationships *are*, how they function, what to anticipate, how to conduct them."[6] In coming to understand this, it's no wonder why we've found ourselves intolerant of receiving healthy love but are inexorably drawn to the chaos and drama of dysfunctional relationships.

Lewis, Amini, and Lannon add,

A baby strives to tune in to his parents, but he cannot judge their goodness. He attaches to whoever is there. . . . Attachment is not a critic: a child adores his mother's face, and he runs to her whether she is pretty or plain. And he prefers the emotional patterns of the family he knows, regardless of its objective merits. As an adult his heart will lean toward these outlines. The closer a potential mate matches his prototypes, the more enticed and entranced he will be—the more he will feel that here, at last, with this person, he belongs.[7]

This gives a clear scientific explanation as to why we enter relationships with people who repeat the destructive patterns we experienced in childhood. Why would children of dysfunctional families, of all people, put themselves in relationship with people who create the same pain they saw firsthand? Wouldn't we be the first ones to run as far from those scenarios as possible? But on a level we aren't even aware of, our brain finds these individuals and kinds of relationships attractive.

This doesn't mean we're to blame for the abuse we may experience in our relationships. We're never responsible for someone else's decisions and actions, especially when it's abusive behavior. Rather, understanding the way our brain works helps us to be more intentional about examining the kinds of relationships we find ourselves drawn to. Understanding this tells us we must exercise discipline and self-control when we find ourselves drawn to someone who relates to us in the same unhealthy ways we experienced as children.

I believe this explanation of attraction also gives credence to the words of the prophet Jeremiah: "The heart is deceitful above all things and beyond cure. Who can understand it?" (Jer. 17:9 NIV). The Hebrew word for *heart* here isn't a reference to the physical organ, or even the seat of our emotions. *Heart* refers more generally to the core of our being, the inner parts of us that we use to determine the trajectory of our lives.

In this proverb, Jeremiah contrasts the mystery of our hearts and the peril of following them with the clarity, confidence, and security that comes from having God determine the trajectory of our lives. This flies hard in the face of the notion that we ought to "follow our hearts." Both science and Scripture tell us that if we aren't careful, our hearts will lead us somewhere we ultimately don't want to go.

Leveraging This Baggage for Good

You may be wondering, how in the world we leverage this baggage for the good of our relationships? There are at least four ways.

Discernment

Because we know we may be inclined toward unhealthy relational patterns, we can be more discerning about what relationships we enter and why. We will enter fewer dysfunctional relationships, and we will better understand why we choose to enter the relationships we do. This is true whether we're talking about romantic relationships, friendships, or even employers.

Therapy

Whether fortunate or unfortunate, Lewis, Amini, and Lannon are very clear that the only way we change our attractors is by having them reformed through consistent engagement in a different kind of relationship. Insight isn't enough. Just because we now understand this about ourselves doesn't mean we can change it. I'll go into more detail in chapter 13 on healthy romance, but for our purposes here, one of the most effective relationships for changing our brain's "relational attractors" is with a counselor or therapist.[8] This isn't strictly romantic attractors, but the kinds of relationships we're attracted to. In the end, as we experience healthy emotional connection, our relational attractors will become more like those of the counselor.

The point in all this is to say that if you're resistant to counseling or fear its stigma, then at the very least, let your desire for better relational attractors drive you to a healthy counseling relationship. The fact of the matter is, we all need therapy or counseling at some point in our lives. It's also true that we won't change as humans until the pain of staying the same is worse than the pain involved in changing. How much pain will you have to endure from staying the same before you're willing to do what's necessary to change?

Relational Intentionality

Passion − Chaos = Romance. Although we discussed the challenges of desiring emotional intensity in our relationships (especially romantic ones), chaos isn't the only way to produce emotional intensity. In fact, one of the great joys of relationships is the emotional intensity they offer. This is the part of the relationship that makes us feel alive. When we discover how to create this desire for passion without the chaos, we can leverage it for good. We create emotional intensity without chaos through relational intentionality.

This can be one of the most powerful ways of producing romance in a relationship.

Chaos uses uncertainty and fear to produce emotional intensity. Romance, however, is when we combine our passion for a person with thoughtful attention to their emotional needs. This also produces emotional intensity. Once we can name that this kind of intensity is a priority for us in a relationship, we can begin to leverage that desire for the good, health, stability, and satisfaction of the relationship. Chaos seeks this emotional intensity at the cost of those things. In fact, it multiplies the joy of a relationship when we can add the security of trust, relational health, and stability to this emotional intensity.

One thing I found most attractive about Sharon when we first met was her incredible consistency. In many of my dating relationships, there was so much guessing about what certain actions or words meant. But with Sharon, anytime I asked her out, she didn't just say no when she couldn't and leave me to wonder what that meant or if I needed to take a hint. Instead, she always offered another time for us to get together. This reassurance freed me from many of the fears and ups and downs of dating and at the same time communicated her desire for me in the relationship. It's not just chaos that can produce powerful emotions in a relationship. They can also come from the security of trust, relational health, and stability.

Authentic Friendship

In nonromantic relationships, a similar principle can still work to produce healthy relationships. Some of us who grew up in dysfunctional families will utilize a particular kind of chaos: *relational drama*. Relational drama gives us the emotional intensity we desire from friends and coworkers. It distracts us from the deeper-seated issues within ourselves that we've despaired of addressing. It may even blind us to the need for this kind of emotional work because relational drama easily disguises our pain as the problems that everyone else creates for us.

When it comes to these non-romantic relationships, the equation is friendship − chaos = relational intimacy. In a dysfunctional relationship, we substitute the emotions of drama for the emotions of relational intimacy. Friendship + chaos = relational drama, and that equation ensures the demise of the relationship.

Because drama is a false form of intimacy, it also produces deceptive forms of positive emotions. In drama, the anger that accompanies accusing someone of betrayal, for instance, drives the sense that a significant relationship in our life has been lost. Whether it's a significant relationship or not, betrayal always intensifies a relationship's apparent importance. This artificially imports a sense of intimacy, without the relational stability and vulnerability necessary for relational intimacy.

Once we discover this kind of pattern, we can use that desire for friendship to drive authenticity, vulnerability, and dedication. These are the elements that produce genuine relational intimacy. In this way, we can let the clear sense of the outcome we want drive our disciplined action in the relationship.

This reverses the course on which we consistently act in destructive ways to produce our desired outcome: emotional intensity. Instead, considering our desired outcome, we conduct ourselves in a way that consistently produces the authentic version of what we want most desperately: relational connection.

Deep Relational Roots

The context of Jeremiah's words about the deceitfulness of the heart is God reprimanding Israel for placing its trust in itself. Israel had made its own ability its strength and withdrawn its heart from submission to the Lord. The Lord goes on to say that the one who trusts in himself "will be like a bush in the wastelands; they will not see prosperity when it comes. They will dwell in the parched places of the desert, in a salt land where no one lives" (Jer. 17:6 NIV).

If we aren't careful, the mantra to follow our hearts can become an excuse to gratify our impulses to disastrous ends. If we're honest with ourselves enough to acknowledge that our hearts may be inclined toward the dramatic and chaotic, we do well to be aware of this and to be more intentional about our relationships.

This is contrasted with someone who trusts in the Lord. This person instead is "like a tree planted by the water that sends out its roots by the stream. It does not fear when heat comes; its leaves are always green. It has no worries in a year of drought and never fails to bear fruit" (Jer. 17:8 NIV).

To all this the Lord warns that we aren't to be lured away by superficial promises; instead, we are to do the hard work that takes our roots deep. In this case, we're talking about relational roots. When these roots go deep, the fulfillment of our relationships won't be subject to the rise and fall of relational temperatures. Instead, our relationships will be sustained by the steady, consistent stream beneath our relational foundation.

When this steady relational intentionality regulates our chaos, we can more effectively utilize another aspect of our good baggage: our exceptional ability to read others. In exploring this next aspect of our good baggage, we will see how the intentional use of empathy can dramatically strengthen communication in our relationships.

10

EMPATHY

Reading People Is Our Superpower

In their book *Overcoming the Dark Side of Leadership*, Gary McIntosh and Samuel Rema share about a young man named William Jefferson Blyth. Billy, as he was affectionately called, grew up in the home of parent with alcoholism. His childhood was tumultuous, violent, and unpredictable. One night when Billy was about nine years old, his mother dressed him up to take him to visit his great-grandmother, who was dying in the hospital.

Billy's stepfather, Roger, didn't want them to go. When Billy's mother said she was going anyway, Roger hauled out a gun and fired a shot over her head into the wall. Billy's mother, Virginia, had no choice but to call the police on her own husband.

This was just one story from Bill Clinton's childhood. A childhood he'd later say was pretty normal. Due to this violent environment, Bill Clinton learned how to read the room and the emotions around him to ensure his own safety and well-being. It also helped him develop the ability to anticipate what others wanted from him.

When it came to Bill Clinton's run for president in 1992, this ability had developed to the point that he was "shading the truth," and what Dan Quayle called "doing a Clinton."[1]

This is not a political statement but an acknowledgment of how our childhood plays out in much larger arenas. As a child of a dysfunctional family, our well-being depended on our ability to read a parent or family member and determine if we were in danger, if we needed to be quiet, if we needed to perform, or if we needed to prepare to receive the inconsistent affection in a way that wouldn't offend the person giving it. Our well-being depended on our ability to assess the emotional climate around us.

Reading People's Minds

Our ability to read our environment works to our disadvantage when we try to read others' minds and discern their expectations of us. We allow what we think others are thinking to dictate our actions and behavior more than being driven by our own internal convictions, emotions, or perspectives and opinions. This can result in the kind of deception we discussed in chapter 6.

It begins by giving different parties what they want, but when those parties become polarized enough, we offer conflicting answers. We may do this without being aware that we're doing it. This is all well and good until those parties begin to talk. Then we find ourselves accused of being two-faced.

The motivation for this kind of doublespeak is innocent enough—just as it was when we started it—we just want to keep the peace. The motivations that drove us in childhood were self-protective. How do I calm, soothe, appease, and de-escalate? We are inclined to use this superpower when we feel most threatened, and when we want to escape conflict.

Good Baggage for the Workplace

What if we could leverage this power of reading people for the good of our relationships? The key is to remember we have this ability even when we aren't threatened. While it's true that this ability activates reflexively in fear, we can engage it in critical relational moments as well.

One area of our lives where we unknowingly use this tool with great frequency is in the workplace. We use it to anticipate what a boss or client wants from us. We use it to determine if they're disappointed with us before they tell us so we can make improvements to avoid any consequences. But what if we could use it for more than escaping punishment? What if we could use it to *produce* healthy relationships in our workplaces? In our professional context, one of the most important assets we have is relational capital. This capital gives us the ability to lead and work alongside others in challenging moments, because the core of relational capital is trust.

Building Trust

Once while I was attending an organizational leadership training, the speaker shared an interesting experiment. Employees were given an image of three X's side by side representing lateral employees, and then one X above those three represented their boss. When employees were asked to circle their team, employees almost exclusively circled the three side-by-side X's, excluding the top X, representing their boss. However, when a boss was asked to circle their team, bosses almost exclusively circled all four X's as representing their team.

The experiment exposed that the bosses and employees saw their team relationships differently. This difference centered around trust. The employees had a high level of trust with one another, but the power gap with the boss created a trust gap. The speaker explained that the most effective way a boss can overcome this trust gap is through communication.

I want to take that a step further to say we overcome the trust gap through *meaningful* communication—that is, communication that expresses a boss's care for their employee beyond simply what the employee can do for them. This superpower of reading people gives us a powerful advantage when we can discern that more is going on for the employee than just their struggling with a project. This doesn't mean invading someone's personal space and privacy, but it does mean recognizing and naming when more is going on than presents itself on the surface.

This emotional sensitivity gives us the relational insight to discern when we might need to say, "Hey, it seemed like you were having a hard time thinking through this project today. Would it help you to go for a walk to clear your mind?" or "It seems you have a lot on your mind today. Would it be better for us to hold this pitch until Monday?" This profound ability to read people allows us to care for those we work with in an unusually meaningful way, and in a way that builds necessary trust for teams to function well regardless of our place on the team.

In Kim Scott's exceptional leadership book *Radical Candor*, she explains that the key to delivering honest feedback successfully is having a relationship in place whereby people also know you care for them personally. People know we care personally when we pay attention to them, take notice of their lives, and ask questions.

This people-reading superpower gives us the advantage of ascertaining the right kinds of questions to ask. We can read emotions through facial expressions with exceptional accuracy. We notice posture, read body language, and measure eye contact and eye movements. And from this, we can discern such perceptive questions as "Susan, I could be wrong here, but it appears you're having some trouble with this proposal. If so, could you share what that is?"

Acknowledging Emotions, Building Culture

Acknowledging emotions does two things for the culture of a workplace. First, it communicates that this is a collaborative effort and dissenting perspectives are not only acceptable but also welcomed and encouraged. Second, it communicates that you care for each team member specifically. It says, "I see you." This is a powerful catalyst for the kind of relational capital that allows a team to go further faster.

William Vanderbloemen's book *Culture Wins* makes the powerful argument that when it comes to teams, culture eats strategy for breakfast. For those of us in leadership roles, few things build stronger culture than our capacity to read people and lead from that. It gives us the ability to discern the emotional climate of a difficult meeting and know where we've pushed far enough and need to stop. It informs us when to pause to address the emotional buildup in the room. It enables us to produce an environment where it's safe to bring our whole selves—emotions, stories, perspectives, and all.

When people know their whole selves are welcome, they bring their whole selves to work. And when we bring our whole selves, we are not only more effective at our jobs but also more devoted to one another. This is our superpower at work.

Good Baggage for Relationships

When it comes to our personal relationships, many of the same principles apply. We can build trust in our relationships by acknowledging and holding space for the emotions of others. We influence the culture of our friendships by inviting others into our emotional world and offering them the safety to share their emotional world with us.

When our ability to read others works with our relational intentionality, we give others the gift of profound empathy. When we empathize, we go beyond reading others. We name pain and validate emotions. This enhances the intimacy established by our relational intentionality and truly capitalizes on our good baggage.

Empathy has been a buzzword of sorts, but it also has been surrounded with much misunderstanding. Simply put, "Empathy is the capacity to understand another's feelings."[2] It's the ability to see an entire situation from another's perspective.

As children, we were forced to see the world through others' eyes and concede to them, lest we suffer for defending our own perspective. This often led to disregard for our own needs. One of our great challenges as adults is not becoming paralyzed by that same empathy. When we are able to understand others' perspectives so well, it can be difficult to enforce our own perspective or make decisions that affect others.

This, however, reinforces the importance of boundaries. Once we understand the limits of our responsibility for the emotions and reactions of others, we can use empathy to our advantage. Because we can so inhabit others' perspectives, we have the exceptional ability to listen to others in a way that makes them feel heard. And they feel this way when we articulate their thoughts and feelings in a way they identify with. This contributes significantly to good communication. And good communication is the bedrock of healthy relationships.

Four Questions

Sometimes it helps to have a framework for the information we gather from reading others. "Four Questions" is one such tool. Four Questions is an assessment tool that can be used to explore our relationships and our interior worlds. The four questions are: *What's right? What's wrong? What's unclear? What's missing?* These questions are especially helpful when we can work through them with the other person in the relationship.

What's Right?

What's right with the relationship? What's going well? It's important to begin here. Naming what's right helps us see that not everything with the relationship is broken. Since our sensitivity is to threats to a relationship, it can be hard to see the things that are going well and need to be celebrated.

What's Wrong?

What's wrong with the relationship? What's broken? This could begin on a very surface level. We're struggling to communicate well. We're having trouble resolving conflict. I'm struggling with jealousy toward this person. I'm having trouble forgiving them. They are angry with me. We had a falling out years ago that we're having trouble resolving. After answering this question, you can utilize the five whys from chapter 1 to go a few layers down and understand the root of the problem. For example, some "first whys" might be: "Why am I struggling with jealousy?" "Why am I having trouble forgiving them?" or "Why are we unable to resolve conflict?"

What's Unclear?

What's unclear is a question to clarify what you or the other person don't know or understand. For example, it isn't clear who's responsible for which chores around the house. It's unclear who pays which bills. It's unclear who's responsible for which tasks on a project at work. It's unclear what their expectations of me are. It's unclear what their preferences are. This could also entail things you're having trouble communicating about.

What's Missing?

Finally, the last question is what's missing? These are things that hurt the relationship by their absence. Examples include trust, respect, boundaries, regular communication, date nights, vacations, boundaries with time, boundaries with work, recreation, rest, and so on.

All these questions can help us get more specific about what exactly the challenges in the relationship are so that you can then address where and what improvements need to be made.

Two Keys to Having These Conversations Well

When it comes to leveraging this superpower in the midst of a conversation, there are two important practices to develop. Both pertain to what we do with the information we ascertain from reading people.

1. Don't Divorce Logic from Emotion

We need to understand on a deep level how impossible it is to divorce our logic from our emotions. The reading of people comes down to reading how emotion manifests itself. After all, it was the emotions of the people in our childhood that scared us, cued us into danger, and gave us the heads-up that things were about to get bad.

But emotion doesn't show up only in anger and aggression. It also shows up in disappointment, discouragement, and disillusionment. Therefore, when we listen, we listen for not only arguments and rationale but also emotional expression, emotional attachment, and emotional investment. We now consider how to acknowledge and honor the emotional component as we respond, regardless of whether we agree or disagree.

I've found that one of the most effective ways to maintain a relationship during a hard conversation is to consider how a statement will be received emotionally, regardless of what the other person may think of it logically. Humility, honesty, conceding perspectives, and understanding go a long way. It's not a matter of knowing when to read emotion. Emotion is always on display.

2. Reading Emotional Climate Change

A step toward honing our reading of emotional expression is learning to be aware of our own emotions rising. It's safe to assume that during an interaction, if we feel our own emotional state changing, the emotions of others in the room are probably changing as well.

Learn to recognize what it feels like when your emotions change. Is it a rising heartbeat, tension in the chest, clenching fists? A major giveaway for me is that my face gets hot. When you notice an emotional change, pivot the focus from yourself to observing others, and practice acknowledging the emotional climate change.

The God Who Listens

In many Christian circles, the notion of empathy is understood as a therapeutic concept that has become a device for justifying sin. When we get inside someone's world and understand it, suddenly sin becomes the pathological response to what others have done to them. This makes others responsible for their disobedience to God's Word and lets them off the hook.

But this misunderstands that the God of the Christian Scriptures is the God who listens. In Genesis 2, God brought every creature to Adam to see what he would call it. In this process, no helper for Adam was found. God saw the situation through Adam's eyes: it was not good for him to be alone. God understood the void Adam felt without a companion. He understood this without having to experience it himself. This is empathy. We're not told whether God and Adam had a conversation about this, but whether Adam explicitly stated it, you could say God "read" Adam and responded by creating Eve, the one who was flesh of his flesh.

God didn't tell Adam to suck it up or take Adam's identification of this need as an affront to his creative capacity. God saw Adam's need and took Adam's experience seriously.

If we fast-forward to Exodus 3, the Israelites had been under the brutal oppression of Egypt for four hundred years. God showed up to a man named Moses in a burning bush and declared, "I have observed the misery of my people in Egypt and have *heard* them crying out because of their oppressors. I know about their sufferings, and I have come down to rescue them" (vv. 7–8, emphasis added). God did not merely hear their cries; he was moved to action. How well we listen is always reflected in how we respond.

In 2 Chronicles 7, God showed up to Solomon and said,

> I have *heard* your prayer and have chosen this place for myself as a temple of sacrifice. If I shut the sky so there is no rain, or if I command the grasshopper to consume the land, or if I send pestilence on my people, and my people, who bear my name, humble themselves, pray and seek my face, and turn from their evil ways, then I will *hear* from heaven, forgive their sin, and heal their land. My eyes will now be open and *my ears attentive* to prayer from this place. (vv. 12–15, emphasis added)

God spoke through the prophet Jeremiah, "You will call to me and come and pray to me, and *I will listen to you*. You will seek me and find me when you search for me with all of your heart" (Jer. 29:12–13, emphasis added).

Finally, when we come to the New Testament, 1 John informs us, "This is the confidence we have before him: If we ask anything according to his will, *he hears us*" (5:14, emphasis added).

This is the God who listens. This is the God who empathizes with us and is moved to action on our behalf. Empathy is not just a therapeutic concept or a tool for good communication. Empathy is essential to God's action toward creation. When we empathize, we reflect God's character as those who bear God's image.

Empathy and Loyalty

As children, we read rooms and assessed emotions. Others' perspectives were forced on us. This caused us to be aware of the pain of others and to disregard our own. But now, with proper boundaries, we can choose when and how to use this superpower to the benefit of our relationships.

But that's not all. The ability to read people well can help us make wise decisions about *who* to be in relationship with. In the next chapter we'll look at another outcome of our childhood: we can be fiercely loyal. Exercising our ability to read people well will help us assess who is worthy of that loyalty in the first place.

11

LOYALTY

Giving Our Allegiance to the Right People

A friend of mine in graduate school grew up in a chaotic home that ended with her parents' divorce. Her parents married after getting pregnant with her and had a volatile relationship, both while they were married and in the years that followed. My friend shared with me often about the conflicted feelings she carried, especially for her father.

The first time I met her father, I was astounded by how lovingly she acted toward him and even how childlike she was in his presence. Her behavior didn't reflect the conflicted feelings she had expressed at all.

As we talked about her relationship with her dad, the reason for her behavior became clear. Regardless of what had happened between her parents, she would never abandon her father the way her mother had abandoned him. Regardless of her own history with her dad and the feelings she had toward him, she would never compromise her loyalty to him.

Where This Loyalty Comes From

Our loyalty first arose as a coping mechanism. This is not surprising. Again, we must honor the work our younger selves did to protect us. We developed this loyalty because it offered us a sense of security in an unstable world.

For those of us who grew up in family systems with alcoholism, Jeff Georgi explains that it plays out this way:

> As they become more enmeshed within the alcoholic system itself, such children can often develop an exaggerated sense of loyalty, if only to convince themselves that they are safe. This exaggerated sense of loyalty may express itself in adult terms, through an inability to break from relationships or situations, even when change or termination is necessary. For some of these adult children even change itself represents a frightening and unacceptable anxiety, which conjures up the dread and uncertainty associated with the addictive system. Many ACOAs [adult children of alcoholics] may put up with unfulfilling or even abusive relationships in order to postpone or avoid change.[1]

Loyalty to the wrong things or to unhealthy relationships was better than the uncertainty of those relationships changing or the uncertainty of what life would be like without those relationships.

Delilah's Gaslighting

In the Old Testament book of Judges, we have one of the most absurd stories of misplaced loyalty in all of literature. A powerful warrior named Samson fell madly in love with a forbidden woman of an enemy nation named Delilah. They embarked on a hidden affair that was eventually discovered by Delilah's people—the Philistines. Samson had a secret. There was a special reason for his power, and the Philistines wanted her to find out what it was.

In the throes of love, Delilah asked Samson what the source of his strength was, and he replied that if he was tied with new bowstrings, he would become as weak as any other man. Delilah acquired new bowstrings and tied him up while he was sleeping. However, when he awoke to an attack from the Philistines, he broke the strings, defeated his assailants, and the source of his strength remained concealed.

Twice more Delilah asked Samson the source of his strength, each time heaping on him the guilt of being dishonest, making a fool of her, and betraying his loyalty to her. If he really loved her, he would trust her. Each time Samson gave false answers to her questions. Each time he was attacked in the middle of the night. And each time he rose to defeat them.

Finally, after three times being told the wrong thing and betraying Samson, she still expected him to be loyal to her. In the end, she asked the very piercing question, "How can you say, 'I love you,' when you won't confide in me?" (Judg. 16:15 NIV). This time, Samson gave her the truth despite her track record for betraying him, sealing his own fate of defeat.

In reading this story closely and through the eyes of healthy boundaries, we might ask who Delilah is to ask Samson this question. It'd be just as legitimate to ask her how she can say she loves him when she has repeatedly betrayed his trust! This is a powerful illustration of the kinds of unhealthy relationships we find ourselves remaining loyal to.

A Disastrous Combination

When this tendency to offer loyalty too quickly combines with our inability to identify healthy boundaries, we confuse unwarranted loyalty with a deep desire to work on the relationship and not give up on it. We see our persistence in unhealthy relationships as good loyalty. We persist in it because of what we perceive to be a commitment to the relationship while disregarding the emotional, verbal, or even physical abuse that's taking place.

To make matters worse, we feel a need to remain in the relationship after it's been detrimental, precisely because it took so much work to get the relationship in the first place.

Leveraging Loyalty for the Good of Our Relationships

One of the most helpful things we can do to leverage this tendency to remain loyal is assess the motivations for our loyalty. Here are some questions to ask yourself to examine why you give your loyalty to the people you do.

Am I loyal because the alternative is too scary?

Are you loyal because the evil you know is better than the evil you don't know? In this scenario, you're loyal because you fear the unknowns of removing your loyalty to this person—or this job, community, or institution. What if life is even worse without them? Based on past experience, you might think that if you got out of this relationship, you'd find yourself in a position worse than the one you're in.

But what if you had more agency on the other side of this relationship to mitigate the evil you didn't know? What if you didn't have to be in a relationship, position, community, or organization worse than the one you're in? Part of the objective of a book like this is for you to discover the things that lead you to those unhealthy relationships so you can avoid them in the future.

Do I feel like I owe this person loyalty for something they did for me?

Do you feel like they've done something for you that you now owe them your loyalty? Do they hold it over your head as a guilt trip for why you should be loyal? When they cross a boundary or treat you poorly, do you tell yourself you owe them your loyalty anyway?

Am I making excuses for others' behaviors that should make them unworthy of my loyalty?

The decision to retract your loyalty is an uncomfortable and even painful one to make. You may attempt to avoid this decision by finding reasons why their behavior shouldn't cost them your loyalty. You may even assume responsibility for their behavior because it's easier to assume responsibility for their doing wrong than it is to hold them accountable for the wrong they've done.

When people—let's be honest, it's my wife, Sharon—call me on this, I often get defensive. This is because I know that what they did was unacceptable, but I don't want to do the more difficult work of confronting them. A previous employee of mine had stopped showing up at Sunday morning services even though he had responsibilities that necessitated his presence. He developed a regular habit of canceling meetings with me at the last minute with no explanation, and he refused to do basic aspects of his job because they just weren't convenient.

Worse, he was unwilling to acknowledge that any of this was a problem. Eventually his changing attitude toward work began to mean additional work for me and Sharon. And yet, every time Sharon asked what I was going to do about it, I found reasons why they didn't show up or why it was okay that they missed that Sunday service or that meeting. Exasperated, she finally asked, "Why are you so loyal to this person?"

The truth of the matter was, I didn't want to confront this person because my loyalty to them was comfortable. It was easier to find reasons to justify their behavior than it was to withhold loyalty and challenge their work habits. I grew defensive with Sharon because I knew that if I acknowledged she was right, I'd lose my own justification for maintaining loyalty to this person. But when I was honest with myself, what made this situation so much more painful was the anger I carried toward myself. I knew deep down that their behavior was unacceptable; I just didn't have the courage to confront them about it.

Am I looking for fault in myself to avoid removing my loyalty?

You may think, *Sure, the person may have done some things wrong, but so have I, and so who am I to remove my loyalty?* This is like the last question, but now you aren't making excuses for them. You're using your own mistakes to lower the bar for who deserves your loyalty. If you can identify all the ways you're undeserving of loyalty, you can then rightly ask, "Who am I to demand such high standards to have loyalty?"

Now, take assessment of the people you are loyal to in your life right now. As children who grew up in difficult circumstances, we often give loyalty very quickly and without a lot of consideration.[2] Maybe this is a gut instinct, and maybe we're often right, but it still deserves reflection. Ask yourself, *Who am I loyal to in my life right now? Are they worthy of that loyalty?*

The truth is, our loyalty is a gift and not everyone in our life is worthy of it. They certainly aren't worthy of it without consideration. The more that we do the work of self-differentiation, and the more we experience the freedom of healthy boundaries and relationships, the more effectively we'll leverage our loyalty for the right relationships and avoid the manipulation of bad ones.

A Particularly Challenging Relationship

When it comes to the question of undeserved loyalty, one of the hardest relationships to break is with a parent or parents. Many of us from dysfunctional families wrestle with whether to remain in contact with parents who continue to hurt us and haven't sought reconciliation through honest confession and repentance.

Two concepts we have already discussed are key in these instances: boundaries and reciprocity. These relationships manipulate us into believing that having boundaries means we are breaking our loyalty. In actuality, what a parent or parents are losing is not our loyalty, but their access to continue inflicting emotional harm on us.

If a parent routinely abuses us verbally, it is not disloyal or unloving to set up a boundary that prevents this disrespectful treatment. It is not disloyal to ask a parent not to drink around their grandchildren. In any such context, their accusation of disloyalty is like Delilah repeatedly calling in the Philistines on Samson but then accusing Samson of disloyalty.

In the same way, reciprocity means that healthy relationships are a two-way street. The same person should not always have to apologize to maintain the relationship. The same person should not always have to concede and sacrifice to make the relationship work. The same person should not always have to absorb the blows. Reciprocity means that if the relationship has been dysfunctional, it is acceptable to ask the other person to sacrifice next time, to apologize before taking the next step with them, or to stop disrespectful behavior toward us or a spouse, child, or others before we reenter the relationship.

If they don't want to meet our requests for respect and reciprocity, they are not interested in a relationship or even our loyalty. What they want is our subservience and servitude.

Delilah after Dark

When I was a kid, there was an evening radio show called *Delilah after Dark*. All I could think about when I heard it was the comical correlation to Delilah's betrayal of Samson, after dark, every night.

We don't know a ton about Samson's childhood, and we want to be careful not to overpsychologize or speculate where the Bible is silent. However, what we do know is that he had a Nazarite vow over his life from a very young age that involved a strict adherence to some particularly religious behaviors. Typically, this vow was voluntary and made from a place of passion and devotion to the Lord.

But for Samson, this vow was pronounced over his life from birth. It would've been a heavy load, and we see how Samson had a difficult time maintaining many of the expectations that came along with it, including not marrying women outside the Israelite people and not eating honey from a dead carcass, which would've made him ritually unclean.

After being involved with several Philistine women, we come to the story we started the chapter with: Samson's irrational loyalty to Delilah. This may not be a story we've ever thought of in terms of loyalty. But all Delilah's manipulations of Samson center on the idea of him not *betraying* her.

When we look to the New Testament and to the life of Jesus, we might ask, What's the difference between Delilah repeatedly betraying Samson and us, as God's people, repeatedly betraying Jesus? Does God allow the same kind of ill treatment without boundaries? Does Jesus die for people who persist in this mistreatment? Aren't we supposed to imitate Jesus? There's so much about the way of Jesus that we're called to follow, including the self-sacrificing nature of his crucifixion.

However, one aspect of the crucifixion that isn't true for us is that Christ's death was the necessary sacrifice to restore our relationship with God. What sets his sacrifice apart is that it was the "once for all" sacrifice (Heb. 10:10). We don't have to continue to make sacrifices for our sins, and we're certainly not making atonement for one another's sins when we choose to endure their treatment and abuse.

Yes, we're called to love. Yes, we're called to sacrifice for one another. But we aren't called to endure someone assaulting the image of God in us. This is where we accept the qualitative difference that Jesus is the only begotten Son of God. This is where we move from imitation to adoration of Jesus.

Jesus is the new and better Samson. Jesus does subject himself to our repeated mistreatment. He does entrust himself to us. But unlike Samson, God's enduring, redemptive power can transform us.

Jesus's sacrifice wasn't out of manipulation and misplaced loyalty. His loyalty wasn't out of self-protection and what he thought this unhealthy loyalty might bring him. He gave his life out of love for the Father and his people.

Loyalty and Our Love for Others

Our loyalty to others really is a gift. It is a gift because in our loyalty, we offer tremendous care to those we love. But when our loyalty combines with our inclination to take responsibility for those we love, it gets really good! That's when our loyalty will drive our love for others in exceptional ways.

12

ÜBERRESPONSIBLE

Caring Well for Those We Love

Everyone wants their Uber driver to be on time. And to know where they're going. My son and I were recently in Chicago for a father-son weekend. As we stood on the sunny steps of our hotel watching cars race down Michigan Avenue, we were looking for our Uber driver's dark-blue sedan. We were headed to the train station for a ride out to the LEGOLAND Discovery Center in Schaumburg. Our driver was late getting to us and then got lost on the way to the station. Yes, you read that correctly. The Uber driver, *with a GPS*, got lost! To make matters worse, in the chaos of rushing out of the car, I left my work phone lying in plain sight on the back seat. We spent half the day traveling around Chicagoland to get it back. Your Uber driver is someone you want to be *über*responsible.

But what about other people in our lives? Is being super responsible ever a problem? It can be for those of us who grew up in difficult circumstances.

In my early twenties, my roommate's friend was coming into town for a long weekend. That Thursday my roommate and I had plans to grab lunch and hit the driving range before he went to pick up his friend at the airport. However, once my roommate caught word that his friend would be landing at five, he canceled the driving range to make sure he would be at the airport when his friend landed. I assured him we would finish at the driving range in plenty of time.

My friend, however, insisted that flights usually come in before their arrival time, which meant instead of landing at five, he would probably land by 4:30. And given that it would be getting close to rush hour, it could take as long as forty-five minutes to get to the airport. This meant he needed to leave by 3:45. And because they were going to dinner as soon as he picked up his friend, he needed to be showered and changed and ready to go by 3:30. And because the driving range was about twenty minutes from our house, hitting balls from two to three would make it impossible for him to get to the airport before his friend got off the plane.

Eventually this led to me asking why it was such a big deal that he be there when his friend *got off the plane*. After all, his friend was a grown man who had been fully capable of getting himself on the plane in the first place. He would be okay if he had to wait by baggage claim for a few minutes.

In digging down a couple of layers in the conversation, we eventually got to his own bad experience. As a high schooler, he had returned home from a trip with his youth group. His parents were supposed to pick him up and were over an hour late. He was embarrassed that his youth minister had to wait with him and hurt that his parents had forgotten about him. The feelings of worthlessness, loneliness, guilt, and even abandonment as a teenager had seared this experience into his memory.

Responsibility was absent from my friend's childhood home. Both his parents struggled with alcoholism, and these kinds of events weren't uncommon. He vowed at that point in his life that he would never cause anyone to feel that way. As a result, in moments like this, it wasn't simply a question of "Could it all fit into that afternoon?" The question was "Did our plans threaten his ability to make good on that childhood vow?"

This situation was deeply emotional for my friend and produced a truly illogical response. But to *his friend*, it was experienced as my buddy being a responsible, conscientious person who honored his commitment to pick him up on time. It is not at all uncommon for children of dysfunctional families to make these kinds of commitments. In fact, our childhood dysfunction can produce a deep sense of responsibility for ourselves and those around us.

The pain we experienced as children forced us to grow by looking inside ourselves for solutions to problems. This work of looking inside of ourselves, though painful, produced emotional maturity as we sought to deal with our strong emotions.

The negative consequence of this, which we discussed in chapter 1, was the way it made us feel responsible for everything. We adult children of difficult circumstances often respond by either internalizing or externalizing—taking all the responsibility for problems on ourselves or putting it all on everyone else. This corresponds to the long-term impact of our childhood, which has resulted in us being either super responsible or super irresponsible.[1]

The super irresponsible among us arrived at the conclusion at some point in our childhood that it didn't matter what we did, things only ever got worse. So what was the point in trying? There was no pleasing our dysfunctional parent(s), so why not just do whatever we want anyway? In this case, our work is to wake up to the reality that not every situation we find ourselves in now is as hopeless as our childhood felt.

Why We Are Super Responsible

There are several reasons why some of us responded with überresponsibility.

We Were Parent-Pleasing

First, we may have become super responsible because as children, we took on more and more in an attempt to please our difficult-to-please parent. We had just enough success to reinforce the belief that if we just kept doing, we would continue receiving approval. However, the intermittent reinforcement drove us to the extreme to maximize the potential for approval, but always with disappointing results.

Everyone Depended on Us

Second, we may carry an intense sense of responsibility because we developed the perception that the well-being of our family depended on us. This could've been due to comments that were made to us about being "the man of the house" because our dad was gone or because we felt the need to protect our younger siblings. This "parental" role distracted us from dealing with our own painful emotions, but it also prevented us from learning to express our own need for help.

The outcome of this is that we developed an identity as a caretaker for those around us. We're most secure in ourselves and feel the greatest sense of value when we're taking care of others.

We Wanted to Avoid Embarrassment

A third reason we've become super responsible is to avoid the embarrassment we felt as children due to our parents' irresponsibility. One of the things I love about my roommate in the story above is that he is the kind of person who is always early and you never wonder if he will be on time. However, the double-edged sword of this is that he becomes intensely anxious and angry when he has to wait for you.

He shared that as a child, he was late to *everything*, and it was so embarrassing. It wasn't the "fashionably late" kind of feeling, rolling in after everyone was already there to celebrate your arrival. It was the embarrassment of coming into a meeting after the conversation had already started, doors creaking and clacking behind you, disturbing the whole room. It was having to apologize repeatedly to teachers and coaches for being late *again*. Given that he had no control over his parents to change this, once he did have control, he vowed it would never happen again.

We Had No Sense of Limitations on Capacity

Fourth, we don't know what normal capacity is, and the drive in us to do whatever it took to please our parents left us with no sense of limitations on capacity anyway. Either because we feared saying no or because having limitations confirmed our own worst fears of worthlessness, we always did more and more. Recognizing our limitations wasn't a question of health but a threat of humiliation. Limitations equaled weakness and inadequacy.

Now, as adults, we're intensely prone to burnout because we don't understand that we all have limitations. More to the point, we refuse to accept that *we* have limitations. Even if we did accept our limitations, we don't know where they are, and we feel guilty for stopping short of overworking for fear that we haven't done enough.

In my own life, I regularly find myself overcommitted or overwhelmed not because I have an overinflated sense of importance but because I don't have a good idea of where my limits are until I hit them. I struggle to take time off because it feels like unless I'm absolutely wrung out, I haven't earned it. I must go into vacation completely exhausted or with a list of recent accomplishments or I don't feel like I deserve it. As a result, I carry a suitcase of guilt with me on vacation as well.

We Had No Experience with Collaboration

Fifth, we had no experience with collaboration. We didn't work together as a family. We didn't have family projects with a plan and assigned tasks through which we learned the power and beauty of interdependence.[2] We didn't learn that it was okay to depend on others. We learned only the pain and punishment of what happened when others depended on us and we let them down. Even worse, we knew the pain of being blamed for the failure of something that wasn't our responsibility. Consequently, we took responsibility for everything to prevent anything from failing and us getting blamed for it.

We Were Out of Touch with Our Bodies' Needs

Sixth, because there was no room for our needs in our childhood, we don't really know when our bodies are trying to tell us to slow down, rest, or take care of ourselves. We don't know our bodies' signals, so we disregard them until they're "blaring alarms"—like panic attacks or heart trouble.

We Feared Saying No

A seventh reason we responded with überresponsibility to our childhood is because we lived in fear of saying no. Saying no might have led to punishment because it was mistaken for disrespect. Today a no might lead to being exposed or "found out." Our inability might expose us as the imposter we are, so we take on more and more, believing we'll prove ourselves if only we do enough. Excessive amounts of responsibility won't change how we feel about ourselves, but they just might convince others to feel differently—better—about us.

We see this play out in profound ways in our professional lives. We appear to be tremendous employees, but we are also a liability because the only time we ever stop is when we get sick.[3] The inability to say no produces burnout because we are unable to assess and execute healthy boundaries. We find ourselves carrying an immense amount of responsibility because we have no sense of our own limitations and no ability to say no even when we feel the physical and emotional strain of taking on too much.[4]

The Cost of Überresponsibility

Some of the most responsible and conscientious people I know are adult children of difficult childhoods. But this can come at the high price of anxiety, perfectionism, and overfunctioning.

Anxiety

The most pervasive impact of super responsibility is anxiety. The correlation of carrying an immense amount of responsibility is the fear of not following through on this responsibility. The fear of not accomplishing all the things we've now taken responsibility for keeps us up at night as we obsess over how to get it all done.

Closely related to anxiety is the concept of "hypervigilance." In hypervigilance, we constantly scan our environment for threats and read other people's moods and emotions. This gives us an edge in preventing mistakes, but it can also cause us to catastrophize, believing the worst thing that can happen will happen.

Perfectionism

It's not enough that we've taken on this responsibility. We must also execute the responsibility impeccably, otherwise the incompetence we live in fear of will surface and expose us. In our work environment, for example, Janet Woititz writes,

> The constant fear of being found out takes much of your energy. It even takes some of the energy that you could be using to do a better job. Not better in terms of what the employer asks for because you're probably giving the employer more than he asks for, but better in being more efficient.[5]

The absurdity of our perfectionism is that we're so afraid of underperforming that we genuinely believe we're on the verge of failure when, in fact, we're most likely far exceeding the expectations of those around us. As perfectionists, we need to develop a fear of burning ourselves out that exceeds our fear of failure.

Overfunctioning

When we overfunction, we take responsibilities that belong to others and make them our own. We do this because we're afraid they won't get it done or won't do it correctly. We *over*function to compensate for others' *under*functioning. This could be because we've seen them fail in the past, or it's simply our anxiety about the negative outcomes if they were to fail. We're especially prone to overfunctioning in our work environments.

In a previous work environment, I had an employee who routinely shirked his responsibilities by exploiting gray areas in his job description. He didn't show up to events for his team because it wasn't required in his job description. It didn't seem to matter that he had responsibilities he couldn't fulfill unless he showed up.

These were responsibilities that any conscientious employee would either assume are entailed in the objectives of their position or would ask for clarification about. However, because I was unwilling to confront the employee, I developed a habit of doing their job for them to ensure the same outcome and to prevent their failure from reflecting negatively on me or the organization.

In the long run, I was simply enabling their irresponsibility and causing myself greater stress rather than forcing them to confront the negative outcomes of failing to own their responsibilities. This kind of overfunctioning is often exacerbated by our codependence, people-pleasing, or fear of confrontation. We know we're doing their job for them, and it makes us so angry. But we're not angry enough to overcome our own people-pleasing or fear of confrontation. So we find ourselves full of resentment on top of the exhaustion from overfunctioning.

How Do We Overcome the Cost of Our Überresponsibility?

If we are going to leverage this baggage for the good of our relationships now, there are two mindset shifts we need to make. You already know these things are true. But sometimes hearing someone else say it helps us to live as though it's true.

Perfect or Pathetic Are Not Our Only Options

It's important to understand and truly believe that being perfect or being pathetic are not our only options. In fact, neither are really options. The truth is, as the responsible people we are, we've never really risked being pathetic even if we were made to feel that way. The fear of being pathetic has driven us so far from it that others probably find our fear of failure ridiculous. Our bigger challenge is coming to grips with the fact that no one is perfect and no one expects us to be perfect except ourselves.

This showed up in a particularly painful way during the pandemic. As the days and weeks went by and the pressures and tensions of life mounted, I struggled to really be present with my kids and intentional about my time with them. I didn't plan out our time well.

As a result, my time with the kids was chaotic, full of them arguing and fighting, and my emotions would erupt because they were an interruption to my life and work. A host of issues needed addressing here, from my career-centered mentality to my poor mental health and emotional well-being. But during all this, I believed that misusing my anxiety medication was the solution to being a better, more present, and relaxed dad.

Once I began meeting with a counselor about my substance use, I learned that we often misuse substances in an attempt to silence shame that we feel whether we're aware of the shame or not.

As I began to reflect on my substance use, I was able to name a significant source of shame in my life: I was afraid I was a bad father. I was repeating some of the same behaviors I'd experienced with my father. The shame of repeating those behaviors was unbearable, and so it was safer to abuse a substance than it was to admit I wasn't the kind of father I thought I was supposed to be.

The work for me was to accept that no father is perfect and to ask for help to be the kind of father I wanted to be. I also needed to understand that just because I wasn't the father I thought I *should* be didn't mean I was the same as my dad. I wasn't the father I wanted to be, but there's always a path of growth, and I realized I wanted to find it and get on it. I wasn't there yet, but this experience showed me that perfect or pathetic were not my only options.

Rightsize Yourself

A major challenge for those of us who grew up in difficult contexts is to see ourselves as neither smaller than we are nor bigger than we are. Given the abuse, condescension, and humiliation we experienced as children, it's difficult not to always see ourselves as the vulnerable, easily broken child whose self-perception was formed and forged in that environment.

However, in our attempt to break free of that perception of ourselves or ensure no one ever treats us that way again, we can project an image of ourselves that's far bigger than is possible for us to be. This is evident in our need to be capable of accomplishing anything and fulfilling any and every responsibility.

Therefore, part of our work will be to move away from seeing ourselves through the eyes of our dysfunctional parent(s). Instead, we need to see ourselves as those we meet now might see us: a full-grown, capable, responsible adult.

Although we may struggle to know what normal expectations of us are, one way we can learn is by having open conversations with trusted friends or counselors about what those expectations might be. The sooner we externalize our assumptions by voicing them to others, the sooner we gain clarity on this issue. Sometimes just saying those expectations out loud reveals their absurdity!

A friend of mine who experienced tremendous trauma as a child will often say things out loud to me for this very purpose. It's absurd that he believed these things about himself in the first place, but saying them out loud helps him understand how unreasonable they are, both by hearing them with his own ears and by me reassuring him that such expectations are unreasonable. He will say things like "So they won't be mad if I don't make it to work on Monday because my grandfather passed away on Friday and I need time to grieve and collect myself?" I have to reassure him, "No, Jeff, they won't. It's normal and reasonable for us to need time to grieve the loss of those we love. You haven't failed your responsibilities if you take time to grieve something that's natural for all of us to struggle with emotionally."

Two Gifts of This Good Baggage

We learn to leverage this inclination toward responsibility well once we can separate responsibility from the anxiety of perfection and the belief that our perfection will give us value. If we haven't attained a permanent sense of value or security from our pursuit of perfection yet, I think it's time we accept that it can't give us that in the first place. This responsible nature can be a gift to our relationships in so many ways once we disarm these crippling ways of living and decouple them from these false beliefs.

The Security You Give Others Is a Gift

One of the great gifts you've surely already seen but haven't been able to fully enjoy is that you care well for those you love. You delight in making sure others are provided for and experience security because of your efforts. You like being the one everyone depends on, and the loved ones in your life cherish that you love them in this way.

You may complicate this at times, however, because the anxiety you carry from finding your identity and value in this role spoils the purity of seeing yourself happy. But know that you can play this role without finding your identity in it. When you do, you will be lighter and those around you will love being with you even more.

Your Dependability Is a Gift

Secondly, your responsible nature is a gift to your coworkers. People love to work with you because they can count on you to get things done. You're a reliable partner and dependable employee. This makes you a strong candidate in any market. However, once you can disentangle yourself from overfunctioning in your work relationships, you move beyond being a good employee and into the realm of an effective, emotionally intelligent leader as well.

Emotional intelligence enables you to see when you're being manipulated by others. As your emotional intelligence develops, you will begin requiring others to do their own emotional work or suffer the consequences of not doing it. Often in work settings, you overfunction because someone has identified—whether knowingly or unintentionally—that your fear of appearing to fail or your need to appear perfect can be used to their advantage. This is emotional manipulation.

As you develop emotional intelligence, you come to see with clarity that this is really about their laziness or their own need to appear perfect. They're using your drive to ensure their own image. Either way, it's good for them to have to deal with their own stuff and it's good for you to be free of dealing with it for them. This, too, is a gift to your coworkers, albeit a much harder one to give them.

Because of our überresponsibility, we care well for those around us, and we care especially well for those we love. This means those we are in romantic relationships with will experience just how exceptional our care for others can be. Whether it's in dating or in marriage, finding fulfilling love comes at the culmination of our relational intentionality, our empathy, our loyalty, and our heart to care for others.

13

HEALTHY ROMANCE

Fulfilling Love in Dating and Marriage

When Sharon and I first met, I thought I was a smooth operator. Sharon, however, was pretty sure this relationship wasn't going anywhere and didn't want to send the wrong message. So, as we finished up dinner on our second date, I took the bill to pay, but Sharon insisted on paying her part. Since we were going to a movie after dinner, I proposed that she cover the cost of the movie tickets to make things even, and she agreed. When we got to the theater, Sharon learned what she didn't know when she'd agreed to pay for the movie tickets—I'd already picked up the tickets before dinner. Like I said, smooth operator.

A few months into our dating relationship, Sharon was going on a trip to Southeast Asia. Since I wouldn't be able to talk to her for a while—you know, this was before Face-Time and video messaging—I decided to gather our previous conversations from our Facebook messages, going all the way back to the first time we messaged each other the day after we met. I compiled them into a bound booklet that I hid in her backpack to discover at the airport or, better yet, on the plane. I could just picture it: the surprise on her face, the gasp of her breath, the tears from her eyes—it was going to be perfect. How could she ever not love me forever now?

The truth behind all this is, I love romance. I love the extravagant displays of affection. I love the rush that comes from creating these kinds of moments. I'm a hopeless romantic. Many of us who grew up in dysfunctional families are.

What Inclined Us to Be Hopeless Romantics?

Growing up in a dysfunctional family, I didn't know what normal love was. I took my cues from TV and rom-coms, which always painted a distorted picture of how effortless and intoxicating romance could be. I became a hopeless romantic because I believed that if we just loved each other enough, that would make everything better. As I watched my parents' marriage fall apart, I developed an infatuation with the idea of love and love being worth it all.

My hopeless romanticism was compounded by a naivete about the challenges of adulthood and parenthood. Despite my father's alcoholism, and in no way am I excusing his substance use disorder, it was only when I became a father that I began to understand how truly stressful parenthood and adulthood could be and why an escape would be appealing at times.

Finally, there may be physiological contributions to our romantic inclinations as well. Research on the nature of human love and childhood development has determined that much of our physiology is on an "open loop." This means our physiology is open to being impacted by those in close proximity to us.

A second person outside of us "transmits regulatory information that can alter hormone levels, cardiovascular function, sleep rhythms, immune function, and more" inside of us.[1] The two of us work in tandem to regulate each other as we transmit this regulatory information.

As we mature, we develop more ability to operate and regulate emotions on a less open loop and to differentiate our emotions from others. Nevertheless, we never operate on an entirely closed loop. We're always transmitting this regulatory information to and from those around us.

The relation to childhood development is that a baby's physiology is "maximally open-looped."[2] A baby hasn't developed any ability to regulate its own emotions and so depends almost entirely on external sources of regulation.

The fact that we didn't receive enough of this external emotional regulation at the early stages of our lives when it was most necessary may well have contributed to our desire for romantic fulfillment. It was necessary because it helped us develop our own internal capacity for emotional regulation. Because we didn't receive sufficient external regulation to develop this within ourselves, we continue into adulthood always looking for external sources of stabilization.

A study with rhesus monkeys—who have a similar limbic brain development to humans—reflects this outcome precisely. Researchers found that when a rhesus monkey was taken away from its mother too early or experienced long periods of maternal absence, it produced a lifelong propensity to despair.[3] This despair is an observable physiological state.

In despair, their heart rates become low and irregular and sleep is lighter, with less REM sleep and more frequent awakenings. The level of growth hormones in their blood plunges, impeding or even stopping their growth.

This is not unlike human children who have had adverse childhood experiences and suffer from a condition known as "failure to thrive."[4] Lewis, Amini, and Lannon contend that limbic regulation explains why. "With less internalized capacity for self-supervision, such a mammal slips precipitously into physiologic chaos whenever his extrinsic source of stability moves out of range."[5]

Researchers conclude that the same consequence is true of human children with erratic mothers. These children tend to be clingy. Lewis, Amini, and Lannon explain that "because they haven't been able to absorb sufficient closed-loop control over their physiology, they need to stay near an external regulator to remain in balance."[6]

Many of us find ourselves to be hopeless romantics because we're desperately in need of an external regulator.

What's the Difference between a Hopeless Romantic and a Healthy Romantic?

Below are some characteristics of a hopeless romantic.[7]

» Our romances ignite quickly and burn out fast.
» We have one-sided relationships.
» We have an overly optimistic view of love.

» We ignore red flags.
» We lead with our emotions.
» We tend to idealize our partner.
» We have a martyr complex.
» We daydream about love.
» We spend all our time with a new partner.
» Love is paramount. It's the most important thing. It's worth sacrificing everything else for.

A prototypical hopeless romantic is Princess Anna from the Disney movie *Frozen*. She daydreams about love, her love with Hans ignites quickly, she idealizes him and wants to spend all her time with him, she ignores red flags, and she refuses to listen to the objective voices who see things more clearly. She's a dramatic example, given she says yes to Hans's proposal the day they meet, but it gets to the point. The problems with this approach to love and relationships are pressed into our faces by their absurdity.

The following are characteristics of a healthy romantic:

» Our romances may ignite quickly, but wisdom keeps a hand on the wheel. Wisdom can be an effective copilot to our emotions as we seek to make better romantic decisions. Andy Stanley has an extraordinary message on applying wisdom in our lives, and it's relevant to romantic relationships as well. The key question is this: "In light of your past experience, current circumstances, and future hopes and dreams, what is the wise thing for you to do?"[8] In light of my past relationship experiences, what's the wise thing to do in this relationship? In light of what's going on in my life right now, what's the wise thing to do in this relationship? In light of where I hope to be in my life in five, ten, or fifteen years, what's the wise thing to do in this relationship? The healthy romantic uses this question to think clearly when emotions are running high.

» We give sacrificially to the relationship, but not in such a way as to make the relationship one-sided. This means we require the other person in the relationship to hold up their side. We prevent our own martyr complex by having limits on what we'll give without reciprocation.

» We pay attention to red flags. We don't make excuses for them or create narratives that explain them away.

For the hope*less* romantic, the objective is to be loved like we see in the movies. For the healthy romantic, the objective is a healthy love relationship.

The mindset of this book is what sets the healthy romantic apart: the growth mindset. The growth mindset says that every challenge is not an indication of our limits but an opportunity to grow.

This may be a mindset that comes more naturally to the internalizer who is always looking for ways to better themselves. But it's a mindset we can all have when it comes to relationships, especially romantic ones. A growth mindset sees each relationship as an opportunity to grow in our relationship ability. The challenges in a relationship aren't necessarily the limits of the relationship or its end, but they are an opportunity to make it stronger.

How We Were Uniquely Prepared to Be a Healthy Romantic

Before we get into how we heal and recover from our hope-lessly romantic nature, I first want to clarify why we're uniquely prepared to be healthy when it comes to romance.

We're uniquely prepared to be healthy romantics because we've seen the pain of moments when the right words or actions could've changed everything, but our parents didn't say those words or take the correct action. As we discussed in the chapter on pursuing relational health, pain is a powerful motivator to confront the pride that prevents us from using the right words and actions now.

I remember the day my dad moved out for the last time. With tears in his eyes, he told me he didn't want to leave, but my mom wouldn't let him stay. I knew that wasn't true. My mom wanted him there. But more importantly, she wanted him to get help for his alcoholism so he wouldn't drive under the influence and put us in dangerous circum-stances anymore. He had left her to choose between pro-tecting her children or continuing to try to "love" him to healing.

As a thirteen-year-old boy, I thought to myself, *Dad, just put it all down. Tell her you will do whatever it takes to make it right. Do the big romantic gesture. Promise her you will change and then start doing it. You don't have to leave. She's not making you leave. You put yourself in this posi-tion. Your own choices are driving you out the door, but they don't have to. Just do the right thing!*

Of course, he didn't—because alcoholism is so much more than a choice. I know that now. But the image of a moment when the big romantic gesture might've brought change inspires me to seize these opportunities rather than seizing my ego.

How Do We Become a Healthy Romantic?

Becoming a healthy romantic has less to do with being romantic and more to do with being healthy. In *A General Theory of Love*, Lewis, Amini, and Lannon offer a three-part healing process comprised of limbic resonance, limbic regulation, and limbic revision. This process heals the relational attractors we formed during childhood by transforming the neural connectors that house these attractors.

Limbic Resonance

Limbic resonance is a term that describes the human experience of connecting on a deeply emotional level with another human being. But this isn't merely an emotional connection. It has a deeply physical aspect to it as well. In every environment, we broadcast information about ourselves and our inner world. As this information is transmitted and received, it affects the physical makeup of our brain.

These are ancient mechanisms built into the very physical structures of our limbic brain. As a result, "These limbic processes [are] as corporeal as digestion or respiration."[9] This is what makes transformation in therapy possible. "Without the physiologic unity limbic operations provide, therapy would indeed be the vapid banter some people suppose it to be."[10]

The point is, this human-to-human connection in psychotherapy does its therapeutic work not only by giving us insight about ourselves; it works by reforming the relational patterns of our brain. It's why even a brilliant therapist who refuses to engage emotionally leaves clients feeling as though they didn't connect. It's because this limbic resonance wasn't given a chance to develop, and the client left with some of their painful patterns reinforced.

However, if a therapist takes the time to hear stories, express empathy, and communicate understanding, the therapist not only gains a sense of this person's inner world but also paves a quite literal highway into their emotional world. The client now feels as though the therapist has worked to inhabit their emotional world with them. The therapist has not merely catalogued information, the patient and therapist have developed a resonance between the limbic regions of their brains.

Limbic Regulation

Limbic resonance paves the way for a second healing mechanism—limbic regulation. Even if you've never heard of the concept, you have certainly experienced it and most likely attempt to create it on a regular basis. Let me explain.

I regularly find myself ruminating on problems or painful circumstances, mulling them over in my mind, ultimately allowing my greatest fears, worries, and discouraging thoughts to run wild. But when I finally take the time to connect with a friend or counselor and share what's going on inside, I almost inevitably leave calmer and more at ease.

You know the feeling. That good feeling you have leaving a conversation with a close friend who just "gets you." Lewis, Amini, and Lannon observe that "people who need regulation often leave therapy sessions feeling calmer, stronger, safer, more able to handle the world. Often they don't know why."[11]

We leave these conversations feeling better because our own emotional world has been balanced through our limbic brain's connection with another human. Our human physiology experiences a centering effect as it engages in harmonizing activity with nearby limbic brains. "Our neural architecture places relationships at the crux of our lives, where . . . they have the power to stabilize."[12]

This isn't unlike our body's alignment with the light of the sun and its circadian rhythms. Like the light of the sun, close relationships produce an orienting, stabilizing effect in a physical but intangible way. All this enhances the tremendous power of human relationships.

Limbic Revision

The upshot of this limbic connection is ultimately to access and transform the neural connections that house our attractors and dictate our relationships. This is the aim, because in light of how our childhood formed our attractors, we simply can't will ourselves to desire a different kind of relationship.

The relational connections of our childhood formed our brain to be attracted to similar kinds of relational connection in the future because of their familiarity. We will continue to be unconsciously attracted to those kinds of relationships, even if we know better intellectually. It's been said that the heart wants what the heart wants. But really, the heart wants what it was trained to want, and it won't change until we've had enough engagement with a healthy individual—a therapist or otherwise—over a long period to transform our native attractors into new ones.

Because of our "emotional mind formed within the force field of parental and familial Attractors, . . . a patient's Attractors equip him with the intuition that relationships feel like *this,* follow *this* outline."[13] For this reason, the most powerful work that a therapist does, over and above any insight they could ever offer, is enter into the kind of relationship that conforms to the client's notion of how a relationship works and feels—not artificially, but in a way that evokes authentic emotional responses.

Over time, as a healthy therapist interacts with the client, the client's native attractors will become more like those of the therapist. This happens because new neural patterns are encoded over the repetition of their connection, and these patterns are fed "limbic nutrients" with each successive connection. With enough time and engagement, the new patterns are fortified and new attractors are solidified.[14]

I go into the weeds of all that to help us understand how we can both experience healing ourselves and be a source of healing for others. This is especially the case in romantic relationships where our lives become intimately entangled. If repetition of engagement with healthy individuals revises our misformed attractors, who can we better love and serve in this way than our life partner? This, of course, assumes we've experienced this limbic resonance, regulation, and revision.

This sets us up well to be transformed from the hopeless romantic to the healthy romantic and to make our partners healthier by being in relationship with them.

Don't Forget!

1. Not every person who gives us attention deserves our romance. This sets a healthy romantic apart. We no doubt esteem love, but not at the cost of self-respect. As I've said, it's not selfish to respect yourself. A healthy romantic holds the value of love alongside the value of wisdom to assess to what degree there's hope for a healthy relationship. For this reason, as a healthy romantic, we will hold out for a love that's going to meet our high expectations.

2. *Don't mistake emotional intensity for meaningful love.* We've already discussed our desire for emotional intensity, but this alone can't sustain a meaningful, life-giving relationship. For this reason, John Gottman, founder of the Gottman Institute, makes the case most forcefully that the foundation of any healthy, sustainable romantic relationship must be friendship. More than compatability and good communication, more than passionate love lives and shared interests, friendship is what sustains romance.

In his book with Nan Silver, *The Seven Principles for Making Marriage Work*, Gottman defines this friendship as "a mutual respect for and enjoyment of each other's company."[15] They know one another intimately. "They have an abiding regard for each other and express their fondness not just in big ways but through small gestures day in and day out."[16] This friendship fuels the flames of romance. Friendship is what provides the positive sentiment between two people to overcome the inevitable tension of relationships.

Psychologist Robert Weiss first coined this concept of Positive Sentiment Override, or PSO, at the University of Oregon. PSO means the positive thoughts that a couple has for one another and their marriage "are so pervasive that they tend to supersede their negative feelings."[17] This positivity gives them optimism about the relationship and their future lives together and encourages them to be gentler toward each other in conflict.

In a shocking statement from a marriage expert, Gottman explains that most marriage conflicts cannot be resolved. That's because most of a couple's "disagreements are rooted in fundamental differences of lifestyle, personality, or values."[18] It's only when a couple develops the mutual respect and honor for each other to live with these differences that they experience meaningful love. Meaningful love comes not from changing our partner into the ideal person we *can* love but by sharing the respect and mutual appreciation necessary to found a friendship and fuel a romance.

Healthy Romance over Rom-Coms

In most cases, healthy romance makes for bad romantic comedies. The hallmarks of rom-coms are the arrogance of one or both of the main characters, a disdain for love from at least one character, misunderstandings driven by poor communication, and the pain of past romantic failures.

In contrast, a healthy romance is characterized by humility. Those in a healthy romance know love is more than just emotional intensity or sexual attraction. They understand that making someone feel understood directly correlates to the level of our intimacy, and healthy romance makes the people in the relationship healthier.

One of the most commonly read Scriptures at weddings is Ruth 1:16: "For where you go I will go, and where you lodge I will lodge. Your people shall be my people, and your God my God" (ESV). What many don't know is that this wasn't spoken in the context of a romantic relationship; it was a friendship between a mother-in-law and her daughter-in-law. Yet for those who are aware of this context and still use it for their ceremonies, it captures a sense of dedication and commitment that every marriage ought to aspire to. The commitment described in Ruth 1:16 isn't the limited dedication of infatuation. It's the wholehearted fidelity of friendship.

PT 4

HOW TO PUT IT ALL TOGETHER

By this point, you've done some hard emotional work. Maybe the hardest you've ever done. As a result, I hope you're beginning to see the impact of your childhood in a new light. I hope you're encouraged by the good that's been packed in your baggage.

But the journey's not over. We've got two more chapters to help put all this together.

We're going to explore how relational formation affects us, down to our personality and brain chemistry. This will help you know what work *you specifically* can do and how.

At the end of this section, you'll understand yourself, your relationships, and where you need to do your own work with renewed clarity.

14

OVERCOMING OBSTACLES TO HEALTHY RELATIONSHIPS

Do we want to live a better life, or do we allow what others did to us to determine the quality of our lives for us? Our dysfunctional family may have taken our childhood from us, but do we hand them our adulthood as well?

We can't change what happened, and we can't change the fact that some of those wounds will be with us for life. But we can choose what we do in response to those wounds. We can choose whether we take responsibility for healing them to the degree we're able.

Will you do whatever it takes to have better relationships, no matter the cost?

The Pursuit of Wisdom and the Benefit to Our Relationships

> If you are wise, you are wise for your own benefit;
> if you mock, you alone will bear the conse-
> quences. (Prov. 9:12)

As much as following Jesus isn't about pursuing ends for our own advantage, Scripture frequently reasserts that wisdom is one thing that, as we pursue it, is to our benefit and to the benefit of those around us. Conversely, if we neglect this pursuit of wisdom, we hurt ourselves and those we love most.

The Hebrew word for wisdom literally translates as "skillful." Pursuing wisdom in our relationships means seeking to relate skillfully with one another. In doing so, we make ourselves lifelong learners in the dynamics of good relationships. We don't arrive in this endeavor. We're always on our way to better relationships, even as we increasingly enjoy the benefits of better relationships.

When the author of Proverbs contrasts the wise person and the foolish person, what distinguishes them may not be what we think. Proverbs 12:15 tells us that the fool thinks their own way is right, but the wise one listens to counsel.

The author is getting at the counterintuitive idea that what characterizes someone as wise or foolish isn't how much wisdom one has but how willing they are to seek it. The wise person is willing and eager to seek wisdom.

Solomon, who wrote much of Proverbs, is thought to be one of the wisest people who ever lived. And yet he advises above all else, and more frequently than all else, that we seek wise counsel.

It's so simple but also so profound. The wise one seeks wisdom, the fool doesn't—and his relationships suffer for it. What this tells us about our relationships is that we can ignore the work of overcoming the obstacles to healthy relationships imposed by our childhood, but we do so to our own detriment. In doing so, we punish not only our relationships but also ourselves. When we choose the path of wisdom, we benefit both our relationships and ourselves.

Internalizers and Externalizers

A crucial element in overcoming obstacles is understanding whether we tend toward "internalizing" or "externalizing." When it came to the problems of our childhood, our general response fell toward one end or the other of this spectrum.

Those of us who are internalizers tend to assume that when something is wrong in our world, it can be fixed by working on ourselves. As children, we assumed we were the cause of all the problems, and the answer was for us to fix ourselves. If we could be a better son/daughter, student, athlete, musician, performer, artist, dancer, then maybe we could make everything okay.

Those of us who are externalizers tend to assume that our problems are because of everyone else. If everyone else would get better, things would be fine for us too. As children, the pain of what happened at home combined with an inability to meet our parents' unrealistic expectations. This combination drove us to act out in ways we couldn't understand at the time. All we knew was that if things were better at home, we might not be this way.

Now, as adults, internalizers assume all the responsibility. Externalizers assume none of it.

This was the first explanation that really made sense of the radically different responses that even children from the same broken home have to dysfunction. It explains why some adult children respond by becoming super responsible while others become super irresponsible.[1]

Those of us who are internalizers took responsibility for every possible thing, believing if we could fix it, everything would be okay. Those of us who are externalizers assumed the problem was everything going on outside of us. If everyone else would get their junk together, everything would be okay. Clinical psychologist Lindsay Gibson writes, "Children who are internalizers believe it's up to them to change things, whereas externalizers expect others to do it for them."[2]

Gibson provides this exceptional diagnostic to help us identify where we fall:

Internalizers

» Internalizers are mentally active and love to learn things.

» They try to solve problems from the inside out by being self-reflective and trying to learn from their mistakes.

» They're sensitive and try to understand cause and effect.

» Seeing life as an opportunity to develop themselves, they enjoy becoming more competent.

» They believe they can make things better by trying harder, and they instinctively take responsibility for solving problems on their own.

» Their main sources of anxiety are feeling guilty when they displease others and the fear of being exposed as imposters.

» Their biggest relationship downfall is being overly self-sacrificing and then becoming resentful of how much they do for others.

Externalizers

» Externalizers act before they think about things.

» They're reactive and do things impulsively to blow off anxiety quickly.

» They tend not to be self-reflective, assigning blame to other people and circumstances rather than their own actions.

» They experience life as a process of trial and error but rarely use their mistakes to learn how to do better in the future.

» They're firmly attached to the notion that things need to change in the outside world for them to be happy. Externalizers believe that if other people would give them what they want, their problems would be solved.

» Their coping style is frequently so self-defeating and disruptive that other people must step in to repair the damage from their impulsive actions.

» They depend on external soothing, which makes them susceptible to substance abuse, addictive relationships, and many forms of immediate gratification.

» Their main source of anxiety is that they will be cut off from the external sources they depend on for their security.

» Their biggest relationship problems include being attracted to impulsive people and being overly dependent on others for support and stability.[3]

Because internalizing and externalizing work like a spectrum, the objective is to learn to internalize and externalize to the right degree at the appropriate times. This means being able to see when we should take responsibility for brokenness in a relationship, and likewise to see clearly and accurately when the brokenness isn't ours to take responsibility for.

When we choose not to do this work, we perpetuate the cycle we're so accustomed to: externalizers will "keep acting up until somebody steps in to help them" and "internalizers may suffer in silence and continue to look just fine, even as they're breaking down inside."[4]

What's Your Work If You're an Internalizer?

Those of us who are internalizers live under the tyranny of pressure, guilt, and unrealistic expectations. As we do the work to become more aware of our inclination to internalize, we will find freedom from its oppression in our lives.

Externalize More

The work of the internalizer is to learn to externalize more often. In fact, the key for both the internalizer and externalizer will be finding a greater degree of balance between internalizing and externalizing.

As the internalizer, you're not the root cause of brokenness in every relationship you're part of. That's true even if others have a profound ability to make you feel this way. Your objective is to develop the ability to see situations clearly enough to name when a problem truly is yours to fix and when it's not.

This kind of book is naturally going to appeal more to the internalizer. The internalizer's natural inclination is to pursue self-improvement. However, this inclination isn't always virtuous.

Often, my own self-improvement has been driven by a sense of inadequacy or the feeling that what's wrong with a relationship is something wrong with me. If I can fix what's wrong in me, then that will fix the relationship.

Because I'm a pastor who's also an internalizer, my inclination when something goes wrong in a relationship with someone in my church is to assume I've done something wrong and I need to fix it. In other words, I internalize the problem and assume that the solution is for me to do something better.

This creates an immense amount of pressure on me and a self-defeating sense of myself. More importantly, it's just not true that I'm always the problem. I've found immense freedom and psychological relief in coming to understand that I didn't do anything wrong; maybe we just disagree. Or maybe the other person is going through something and the pain in them is expressing itself through frustration toward me.

Practice Self-Differentiation

As we discussed in chapter 1, differentiation is the ability to remain relationally close to others without allowing your own emotional life to be significantly impacted by them. Given that we, as internalizers, tend to make every problem our responsibility, it's extremely difficult not to make others' emotional troubles ours to fix. It's also difficult for us to see other people upset and not assume that somehow we're responsible for their emotions.

As a pastor to young adults, I carried immense amounts of anxiety going into Sunday mornings. As I worked to mine the causes of this with my counselor, we discovered that my anxiety came from seeing the parents of the twentysomethings I was responsible for. I was anxious because I correlated their emotional state with their assessment of my job performance. If they were happy, they must have been happy with how I was ministering to their adult-age kids. If they were avoidant or distant or vaguely not enthused to see me, it must have meant they were disappointed in me.

During one conversation, my counselor said to me, "No offense, Ike. You just aren't that important." Originally, I was a little offended. "Of course I'm that important," my ego protested. But she was exactly right. These parents had a thousand things more pressing on their minds than to assess my recent job performance. Their facial expressions most likely had very little, if anything, to do with me.

Though humbling, my counselor's comment set me free from interacting with these parents based on my interpretation of their emotions. I could now differentiate myself enough from them to greet them as I would anyone else on Sundays. I could now assume that if they had a problem I needed to take responsibility for, they'd have the maturity to seek me out to discuss it.

You can begin this work of self-differentiation by asking questions like:

> » Is it possible that something else may be contributing to their poor emotional state?
> » What might be going on in their life that's contributing to problems in the relationship?
> » What have I taken responsibility for fixing that I haven't been asked to fix?

» Has this person told me they are upset with me, or am I assuming they are?

» Can I hold off on taking responsibility for this problem until I am asked to (even if they are passive-aggressively trying to "tell" me this)?

Learn about Relationship Dynamics That Make You Feel like You're the Problem

There are several relationship dynamics that can make us feel like we're responsible when, in fact, we're not.

Triangulation

Triangulation occurs when two people in a relationship collude against a third, or when one person co-opts an outside person into a two-person relationship. In both cases, if you're the third party or the one co-opted into the relationship, you may feel responsible for something the other person should take care of themselves.

Some examples of triangulation you might be familiar with include the following:

» "Jeff didn't do this for me, and he said he would. Can you talk to him? I think he'll listen to you better than me."

» "I'm not the only one who feels this way. Leslie and her family told me they feel the same way."

» "I'm just telling you what Will said."

» "Shannon and I talked about it, and we think you should . . ."

» "Kara said Stephanie didn't invite her to the event. Can you talk to her about it and see why?"

Often in such instances, you suddenly become responsible for something that, if you now refuse to fix it, makes *you* the bad guy.

In his extraordinary book *Managing Leadership Anxiety*, Steve Cuss explains that "people who struggle with direct communication are particularly prone to triangulation because co-opting people onto their 'team' is a way they overcome their feeling of powerlessness."[5]

As strange as it sounds, one relational dynamic that makes me feel like I'm the cause of problems I'm not responsible for as a pastor is when a couple triangulates me into their marriage. When there are problems in a couple's relationship and they're having difficulty connecting with each other, couples will bond over their frustration with me as the pastor.

Until I began to externalize and understand what was happening, I wore myself out trying to understand what I needed to do differently to make them happy. As soon as I fixed one thing, something else would be a problem. Their relationship with each other needed the false form of intimacy that came from their shared frustration with me. Once I began to externalize, I found a healthier perspective on these relationships and my role in fixing them.

Conflict Avoidance

When we are conflict avoidant, we tend not to tell others when they've hurt us. This compounds the pressure we feel to fix the situation on our own. The obvious problem is, we are trying to fix their hurtful behavior without acknowledging *their hurtful behavior*. We attempt to fix their behavior with our own. When our attempts fail, we blame ourselves.

Scapegoating

Scapegoating occurs when we are in relationship with someone who projects the problems of the relationship onto us. In these situations, we have two people explicitly making us responsible for the problems of the relationship: ourselves and the person projecting the problems onto us. This is especially destructive if we are conflict avoidant.

What's Your Work If You're an Externalizer?

If you're more of an externalizer, your work will be to develop a greater ability to look inside yourself for solutions to relational brokenness. This means instead of assessing how everyone else is messing up your life, you ask yourself some tough questions.

> » *How have I contributed to the problems in my relationships?* Our tendency might be to disregard our contribution to the problems because it feels insignificant compared to what the other person has done to break the relationship. This, however, is our perception. We're working to perceive situations more accurately and to take responsibility where it's needed. *Important note*: We're not talking about instances of abuse, including justifying abusive behavior by acknowledging what we might've done to deserve it. There's no justification for any kind of

physical, sexual, verbal, or emotional abuse of any kind—ever.

» *What work can I do in myself to improve the quality of my relationships?* Whether at work, at home, with friends, with roommates, or in romantic relationships, ask yourself the following questions: Do I need to improve my communication? Do I need to become less defensive? Less critical? Less reactive and explosive? Do I need to become more emotionally available? More physically present? Do I need to grow in my ability to see situations from other people's perspectives?

» *Have I caused the very reactions in others that I blame them for?* As externalizers, we "engage in behaviors that often exasperate and anger others."[6] As a result, we drive away the very people we need help from. If we can't see this, we'll blame them for abandoning us when, in fact, our own reckless behaviors drove them away in the first place.

» *What's my stress trying to tell me?* As externalizers, we may short-circuit our own growth because we rush to relieve our stress as soon as we feel it. Because we believe someone else needs to solve our problems, we look to others to make us feel better. We grow when we do the introspective work to ask what we can do differently to relieve our own stress.[7] We can also recognize the sources of our stress and do the work necessary to avoid finding ourselves in the same position again. Chances are, we've been here before. We just blamed a different person for taking us back to the same place. It's time to recognize the common denominator here.

If you're an externalizer, your work is to begin finding ways of taking responsibility for your relationships and, in particular, the challenges you repeatedly face in them.

Twelve-step programs, for example, could be thought of as assisting externalizers in taking more responsibility for their lives, the destructive impact they've had on the world around them, and the brokenness in their relationships.[8]

If you often find yourself in different relationships that are falling apart for similar reasons and you always blame the other person, it might be time to look inside yourself and examine how you could be contributing to the brokenness as well.

Genogram

Whether we tend toward internalizing or externalizing, the genogram is a powerful tool for overcoming obstacles to exceptional relationships. A genogram is a map of our family tree that pays particular attention to the nature of the relationships back two or three generations.

This develops a picture of our family dynamics to understand the generational impact of dysfunction. It entails building out a family tree and then diagramming where relationships were broken and where dysfunction existed: Was there abuse? Mental illness? Substance use? Divorce?

This tool is also extremely helpful for placing our parents in context. What dynamics did they grow up in that contributed to their obstacles to having healthy relationships?

What dysfunction did they survive that contributed to the dysfunction of our family?[9]

Disarming Switches

Much of the work of overcoming the kinds of obstacles discussed in this book pertains to disarming switches and triggers in us that we assumed were normal human reactions. In reality, these were born out of particular experiences. Once we understand these pain triggers and switches, we'll be able to disable them and leverage the good baggage packed in them for the good of our relationships now.

15

LEVERAGING YOUR BAGGAGE FOR THE GOOD OF YOUR RELATIONSHIPS

If you take nothing else away from this book, I want you to know that bad relationships in your childhood don't predestine you to be bad at relationships yourself. You have so much more to offer than you may have ever realized, and certainly more than you've been led to believe.

The Resurrection and Redemption of Good Baggage

When it comes to the death and resurrection of Jesus, the resurrection wasn't a foregone conclusion. No one expected him to rise from the dead. The same could be said of our stories. Dead people stay dead and broken people stay broken.

What's counterintuitive about this book is the same thing that was counterintuitive about the resurrection: our greatest defeat became our greatest opportunity. Ernest Hemingway put it well when he said, "The world breaks everyone and afterward many are strong at the broken places."[1]

What made the resurrection so powerful is the fact that it was not what happens to dead people. God's Spirit gives us the same thing he gave the resurrection: the power to do something that humanity doesn't have the power to do on its own. This book isn't only an invitation to reverse the impact of our childhood. It's an invitation to experience God's healing and transforming work in us.

In the Christian tradition, we have this notion called sanctification. Sanctification often gets built up into this sense of being super holy and legalistic. But sanctification is really a notion of healing—the process of being healed back to the kind of human we were created to be in the first place. In this regard, Jesus isn't only the true God; he's also the true human—the kind of human we're invited to be again.

This is where we get the traditional language that sanctification means progressively being transformed to be more like Jesus. God does this work in us for the sake of what he wants to do through his people in the world. God wants to use his people to make the world a more just, equitable, and peaceful place. But this work isn't only good for the world. It's also good for us. Life is better—not *easier*—but better when we live it the way Jesus as the true human did.

In the same way, relationships contribute significantly to our peace, joy, and contentment. For this reason, learning to leverage the good things our childhood put in us is good for our relationships. It's also really good for us.

One of my ongoing challenges is my tendency to get defensive. Working to become less defensive is good for my relationships and helps prevent frustration and tension. But being less defensive is also really, really good for me. When we see this work in light of how good it is for us, we engage it with renewed passion and enthusiasm.

The Fruit of the Spirit and the Fruit of Our Baggage

In the Christian Scriptures, the book of Galatians talks about the fruit of the Spirit (Gal. 5). Like an apple on a tree, the fruit of the Spirit is the observable expression of the invisible work God's Spirit is doing inside us. When we think of this fruit of the Spirit, we tend to think of it as something that shows up in our lives almost randomly and instantaneously.

We forget that fruit in the natural world is the product of a long process that takes place beneath the surface of the soil. First the tree must develop roots, sprout a trunk, grow branches, and produce leaves. The tree then uses those leaves to transform sunlight into food and takes nutrients from its roots to finally produce its beautiful fruit.

The work of the Spirit in our lives also produces beautiful fruit, but in the same way, it's not random or instantaneous. It's the fruit of the Spirit's *work*. The Spirit does work beneath the soil of our hearts and minds, taking broken pieces, taking things that have died.

The Spirit uses this organic matter of our souls to build a new core to who we are. The Sprit builds a strong trunk to support branches and leaves that can produce nutrients before the beautiful fruit finally emerges. The fruit of love, joy, peace, patience, kindness, goodness, faithfulness, gentleness, and self-control (see Gal. 5:22–23).

Our good baggage is also a fruit of the beautiful work that the Spirit does within us. And this fruit isn't instantaneous either. It's the Spirit's ongoing work of taking the broken things in us and healing them. The good baggage we've been carrying produces good things inside us when we allow God's Spirit to transform us in this way.

A Transformed Perspective on Our Baggage

One of the most frustrating aspects of going on a trip is when you lose something in your luggage and have to riffle through it to find the lost item. You know you put it in there, but amid all the clothes, toiletries, books, and whatever else you carry, it's fallen into the suitcase somewhere and can't be found. If you're anything like me, you ultimately end up pulling *everything* out of the suitcase, only to find it lying in the bottom of the bag.

Contrary to this experience, my hope is that you now look at the baggage you carry not as an extra burden but as a bag of potential possibilities. A bag that you're eager to open and riffle through because you might just find something you didn't know was there. Or perhaps something that you had wanted to keep deep down in the bottom but that now has tremendous potential to give life to you and to your relationships.

My hope is that you've come to see yourself as far more than what your pain and experiences have told you that you are. I pray you can now see the good things your difficult childhood put in you. However, this book means very little if you don't put in the work to experience the benefits of your good baggage. It's up to you. There are lots of good things in you. But only you can decide whether to open those bags, pull the pieces out, take the time to assess them, and do the work to redeem them. Your childhood prepared you for exceptional relationships. It's up to you to make them a reality.

Throughout this book I've invited you to think a little bit differently about many of the common obstacles to healthy relationships. The pain of your childhood can benefit your relationships, whether that be with friends or at work, school, or home. The practices and exercises are meant to help you take those steps toward using the stuff that was put in you for your good.

Do You Want to Be Well?

When it comes to taking care of our baggage, I'm reminded of Jesus coming to the pool of Bethesda and seeing the man who had been sick for thirty-eight years (John 5:1–16). Jesus approached the man because he saw that he had been stuck in the same place for a long time. Maybe you resonate with this man?

Jesus approached the man with a profound question, a question I believe he's putting to you and me today: Do you want to be well?

Maybe this isn't the first time you've been asked this question. Maybe like with the man, it's been asked of you before, and like the man, you explained why that just wasn't possible. But Jesus didn't ask if it was possible. Jesus asked the man if he wanted to be well and then instructed him to get up, take his mat, and walk.

Maybe you feel like you've been stuck in the same place for years. Every time you hoped to get well, there was a reason it couldn't work. But like the man at the pool of Bethesda, maybe the question isn't being at the right place at the right time with the right kind of help. Maybe it has more to do with putting forth the effort to get up, take your baggage, and put one foot in front of the other.

Where Do You Begin?

I encourage you to start like the man by the pool did: take one step at a time. Find the concept or idea that connects with you most deeply and begin there. Don't try to tackle it all at once. This is the beginning of a journey. As you take steps forward, your excitement and hope will grow. Every challenge you address will be a powerful motivator to go a step deeper. You will experience change and transformation. Hope will shine in areas of your life that once felt hopeless.

As this transformation takes place in you, you'll feel the impact on your relationships. You'll experience the exceptional relationships you've been prepared for. Don't wait. Take up your good baggage and walk.

ACKNOWLEDGMENTS

Attempting to express gratitude for all those who have made this book possible may be the most daunting part of this whole project. I cannot thank the team at Baker Books and my editor, Brian Vos, enough for believing in this work and the importance of getting its message out into the world. Thank you for taking these ideas and helping craft them into the best book possible!

I would also like to thank Matt Conner, MD, psychiatry; Melissa Brownback, MA, LPCC, LPCC; and Lindsay Geist, MDiv, MSW, LCSW, who all read early drafts of the book and provided invaluable feedback grounded in their areas of expertise. You all helped me avoid flaws in logic and misinformed conclusions. Any such remaining mistakes are due to my own stubbornness in choosing not to accept their recommendations.

Jeff Georgi, AH, LCAS, LCMHC, CCS, CGP, has served both as a counselor and a crucial conversation partner to help grow my understanding of addiction and its impact on family systems. He's an expert in addictive family systems, and I could not be more grateful for his research and the time he has invested in me to aid in my comprehension of these issues. Thank you, Jeff.

When it comes to working through the impact of my own childhood, no one has been more instrumental in my healing and recovery than my counselor, Shannon Plate, MA, LCPC. Shannon has walked with me and Sharon hour after hour, month after month, for the past twelve years. Shannon and I have partnered in ministry endeavors, and her books have been a tremendous resource for me and for the relationships of people in our church. Thank you, Shannon, for the absolute gift you have been to me, my marriage, and my ministry. Your impact on my life is reflected on every page of this book.

I also am deeply grateful to our Bright City Church family, the community that Sharon and I have the joy and privilege of leading. Of all the people whom I hope this book helps, I pray it's most healing for the people of this faith community. As a pastor entrusted with shepherding this specific flock, I do this work first and foremost to see God's healing in you. To this end, I enlist this work as a salve for the pain of all those in our church who experienced a difficult childhood.

Hands down, there is no one more responsible for who I am or what work I do today than my mom, Ellen Miller. Mom, your silent strength and endurance sustained our family through some of the most painful experiences of our lives. It's that same strength now working in me to share these stories in the hope of helping others redeem the kinds of trauma we came to know so well. Thank you for being the mother we needed, for protecting us and loving us enough to make the hard decisions you had to make, regardless of the suffering you had to endure as a result. I hope the words of this book honor the pain you had to carry. I hope you find peace in knowing that though there was much out of your control, you did the unimaginable: you raised three kids who live with a deep faith, follow Jesus with great passion, and fiercely love their mom.

Finally, words seem to fail me in my attempt to capture my gratitude for my wife, Sharon. This book simply would not exist without your undying, unconditional, sacrificial love for me. As the pain of my own story began to surface and spill out into our lives, you did not run from the mess it created. Instead, you waded into the mess with me, hand in hand, fighting for me even as the pain hurt you as well. Thank you for holding me closer, loving me in all the hard ways you had to, championing my healing, and cheering me on. I am simply unworthy of you. Thank you for being the very best part of my life. I love you.

NOTES

Introduction

1. "Defining the Traits of Dysfunctional Families," King University, May 31, 2017, https://online.king.edu/news/dysfunctional-families/.

Chapter 1 Is Anything Ever Really Okay?

1. Andrew Murray, *Humility: The Beauty of Holiness* (Abbotsford, WI: Aneko Press, 2016), 2: "The life God gives is not all at once, but moment by moment, through the unceasing operation of His mighty power. Humility, the place of entire dependence on God, is the first duty of the creature, and the root of every good quality."

2. Murray, *Humility*, 2.

3. Murray, *Humility*, 4.

4. Jane Middelton-Moz and Lorie Dwinell, *After the Tears: Helping Adult Children of Alcoholics Heal Their Childhood Trauma* (Deerfield Beach, FL: Health Communications, 2010), 46–48.

5. This depiction of the cyle of intoxication is adapted from Middelton-Moz and Dwinell, *After the Tears*, 46–48.

6. Middelton-Moz and Dwinell, *After the Tears*, 99.

7. Middelton-Moz and Dwinell, *After the Tears*, 99–100.

8. Taiichi Ohno and Norman Bodek, *Toyota Production System: Beyond Large-Scale Production* (Cambridge: Productivity Press, 1988), 17: "By saying why 5 times, the essence of the issue and its solution become evident."

Chapter 2 What Is a Normal Relationship Anyway?

1. Middelton-Moz and Dwinell, *After the Tears*, 26–30.
2. "Stages of Change," Therapist Aid, 2012, https://www.therapistaid
.com/worksheets/stages-of-change.

Chapter 4 Codependency

1. Tian Dayton, *Emotional Sobriety: From Relationship Trauma to Resilience and Balance* (Deerfield Beach, FL: Health Communications, 2010), 152.
2. Middelton-Moz and Dwinell, *After the Tears*, 170.
3. *Strengthening My Recovery: Meditations for Adult Children of Alcoholics/Dysfunctional Families* (Torrance, CA: Adult Children of Alcoholics World Service Organization, 2013), 144.
4. *Strengthening My Recovery*, 120.
5. Edwin H. Friedman, *A Failure of Nerve: Leadership in the Age of the Quick Fix* (New York: Church Publishing, 2017), 14.
6. Friedman, *A Failure of Nerve*, 14.
7. Friedman, *A Failure of Nerve*, 14.
8. Peter Scazzero, *Emotionally Healthy Spirituality Day by Day: A 40-Day Journey with the Daily Office* (Grand Rapids: Zondervan, 2018), 41.

Chapter 5 Approval Seeking

1. Charles Whitfield, *Healing the Child Within: Discovery and Recovery for Adult Children of Dysfunctional Families* (Deerfield Beach, FL: Health Communications, 2010), 10.
2. Robert S. McGee, *The Search for Significance: Book and Workbook* (Nashville: Thomas Nelson, 1998), 44.
3. McGee, *The Search for Significance*, 85.
4. Robert J. Wicks, *Availability: The Challenge and the Gift of Being Present* (Notre Dame, IN: Sorin Books, 2015), 69.

Chapter 6 Deception

1. Janet Woititz, *The Complete ACOA Sourcebook: Adult Children of Alcoholics at Home, at Work, and in Love* (Deerfield Beach, FL: Health Communications, 2002), 48.
2. Woititz, *The Complete ACOA Sourcebook*, 48.

Chapter 7 Boundaries

1. Henry Cloud and John Townsend, *Boundaries: When to Say Yes, How to Say No to Take Control of Your Life* (Grand Rapids: Zondervan, 2017), 61.

2. Lindsay C. Gibson, *Adult Children of Emotionally Immature Parents: How to Heal from Distant, Rejecting, or Self-Involved Parents* (Oakland: New Harbinger Publications, 2015), 182.

3. Gibson, *Adult Children*, 181–85.

Chapter 9 Relational Intentionality

1. Middelton-Moz and Dwinell, *After the Tears*, 70.

2. Bessel A. van der Kolk, *The Body Keeps the Score: Brain, Mind, and Body in the Healing of Trauma* (New York: Penguin Books, 2015), 188.

3. Thomas Lewis, Fari Amini, and Richard Lannon, *A General Theory of Love* (New York: Vintage Books, 2007).

4. Lewis, Amini, and Lannon, *A General Theory*, 160; Van der Kolk, *The Body Keeps the Score*, 188: "Early attachment patterns create the inner maps that chart our relationships throughout life, not only in terms of what we expect from others, but also in terms of how much comfort and pleasure we can experience in their presence. . . . Our relationship maps are implicit, etched into the emotional brain."

5. Lewis, Amini, and Lannon, *A General Theory*, 160.

6. Lewis, Amini, and Lannon, *A General Theory*, 160.

7. Lewis, Amini, and Lannon, *A General Theory*, 160.

8. Lewis, Amini, and Lannon, *A General Theory*, 187.

Chapter 10 Empathy

1. Paul Fick, *The Dysfunctional President: Inside the Mind of Bill Clinton* (New York: Carol Publishing, 1995), 64.

2. Shannon Plate, *Care Talk: Untangling Great Communication* (self-pub., 2019), 19.

Chapter 11 Loyalty

1. Jeff Georgi, *Adult Children of Addiction: A Population in Need of Definition and Treatment* (Duke Alcoholism and Addictions Program, n.d.), 3.

2. Woititz, *The Complete ACOA Sourcebook*, 276.

Chapter 12 Überresponsible

1. Woititz, *The Complete ACOA Sourcebook*, 71.

2. Woititz, *The Complete ACOA Sourcebook*, 71.

3. Woititz, *The Complete ACOA Sourcebook*, 71.

4. Woititz, *The Complete ACOA Sourcebook*, 71.

5. Woititz, *The Complete ACOA Sourcebook*, 72.

Chapter 13 Healthy Romance

1. Lewis, Amini, and Lannon, *A General Theory*, 85.
2. Lewis, Amini, and Lannon, *A General* Theory, 85.
3. Lewis, Amini, and Lannon, *A General* Theory, 86.
4. Nadine Burke Harris, *The Deepest Well: Healing the Long-Term Effects of Childhood Trauma and Adversity* (Boston: Mariner Books, 2018), 107.
5. Lewis, Amini, and Lannon, *A General Theory*, 86.
6. Lewis, Amini, and Lannon, *A General Theory*, 86.
7. Cristina Montemayor, "11 Signs You May Be a Hopeless Romantic," *Brides* (blog), January 21, 2021, https://www.brides.com/what-is -a-hopeless-romantic-5095882.
8. Andy Stanley, *Ask It: The Question That Will Revolutionize How You Make Decisions* (Portland, OR: Multnomah, 2014), 122.
9. Lewis, Amini, and Lannon, *A General Theory*, 168.
10. Lewis, Amini, and Lannon, *A General Theory*, 168.
11. Lewis, Amini, and Lannon, *A General Theory*, 172.
12. Lewis, Amini, and Lannon, *A General Theory*, 171: "When people are hurting, and out of balance, they turn to regulating affiliations: groups, clubs, pets, marriages, friendships, masseuses, chiropractors, the internet. All carry at least the potential for emotional connection. Together, those bonds do more good than all the psychotherapists on the planet."
13. Lewis, Amini, and Lannon, *A General Theory*, 178.
14. Lewis, Amini, and Lannon, *A General Theory*, 178–79.
15. John M. Gottman and Nan Silver, *The Seven Principles for Making Marriage Work: A Practical Guide from the Country's Foremost Relationship Expert* (New York: Harmony Books, 2015), 21.
16. Gottman and Silver, *The Seven Principles*, 22.
17. Gottman and Silver, *The Seven Principles*, 22.
18. Gottman and Silver, *The Seven Principles*, 28.

Chapter 14 Overcoming Obstacles to Healthy Relationships

1. Woititz, *The Complete ACOA Sourcebook*, 71.
2. Gibson, *Adult Children*, 88.
3. Gibson, *Adult Children*, 89–90.
4. Gibson, *Adult Children*, 90.
5. Steve Cuss, *Managing Leadership Anxiety: Yours and Theirs* (Nashville: Thomas Nelson, 2019), 94.
6. Gibson, *Adult Children*, 90.
7. Gibson, *Adult Children*, 91.
8. Gibson, *Adult Children*, 95.

9. A great resource for developing your own genogram can be found here: https://www.emotionallyhealthy.org/wp-content/uploads/2020/02/GENOGRAM-WORKBOOK.pdf.

Chapter 15 Leveraging Your Baggage for the Good of Your Relationships

1. Ernest Hemingway, *A Farewell to Arms: The Hemingway Library Edition* (New York: Scribner, 2014), 158.

Ike Miller and his wife, Sharon, lead Bright City Church in Durham, North Carolina. He is a North Carolina native who spent just enough time in the frigid Midwest to complete his PhD in theology from Trinity Evangelical Divinity School.

Prior to pursuing doctoral work at TEDS, Ike completed his MDiv at Duke Divinity School, where he and Sharon met. He also did his undergrad degree at a Baptist liberal arts school, which means he is a bit of a theological mutt.

Since planting Bright City in 2018, Ike has served as lead pastor and in the process has learned a great deal about himself, leadership, and most of all, how to establish and maintain emotional and relational health.

After a devasting season of ministry exhaustion, including struggling with and recovering from a substance use disorder of his own, he developed a great passion for helping others who grew up in difficult circumstances to better understand how those environments continue to impact them and their relationships now.

As a pastor, Ike is well aware of the healing work Jesus brings to hurting people's lives. However, he knows firsthand how deeply the coping mechanisms and survival tools of our childhoods are ingrained in us. These subconscious but very real relational habits cannot be healed without being disarmed. We disarm them by coming to understand how they were formed in the first place and how we can reform them now.

Consequently, Ike believes this kind of work is critical for our recovering the kind of healthy relationships we all want but have a hard time finding. Having experienced his own healing through this process, he is passionate about helping others do the same and discover how their difficult childhoods not only wounded them but also worked incredible things into them.

Connect with Ike:
Instagram @IkeFMiller
Twitter @IkeFMiller